W9-AZH-440

Living
KABBALAH

WITHDRAWN

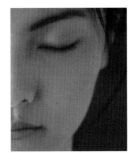

Living
KABBALAH

Maggy Whitehouse

hamlyn

First published in Great Britain in 2004
by Hamlyn, a division of Octopus Publishing Group Ltd
2–4 Heron Quays, London E14 4JP

Distributed in the United States and Canada by
Sterling Publishing Co., Inc.
387 Park Avenue South, New York, NY 10016-8810

Copyright © Octopus Publishing Group Ltd 2004
Text copyright © Maggy Whitehouse 2004

The right of Maggy Whitehouse to be identified as the author
of this work has been asserted by her in accordance with the
Copyright, Designs and Patents Act, 1988.

All rights reserved. No part of this work may be reproduced
or utilized in any form or by any means, electronic or
mechanical, including photocopying, recording or by any
information storage and retrieval system, without the prior
written permission of the publisher.

ISBN 0 600 60970 7
EAN 9780600609704

10 9 8 7 6 5 4 3 2 1

A CIP catalogue record for this book is available from the
British Library

Printed and bound in China

CONTENTS

What is
KABBALAH

Kabbalah is the only complete western mystery tradition and underpins the three main western religions (Judaism, Christianity and Islam). A 'mystery tradition' is the name for the inner – or esoteric – teaching of any particular religion or belief.

Kabbalah is both a path of personal development and a way of understanding how the universe works. Although it is traditionally believed to be Jewish, it in fact pre-dates Judaism – it is said to be as old as humanity itself. It can be practised by anyone seeking a more balanced and happy life, regardless of their religion, nationality, gender or personal belief system. And Kabbalah is now very much in the public eye. The controversial 'Kabbalah of the Famous' has put it on the front page of our newspapers, and many people who are interested in spirituality have begun to investigate Kabbalah.

At first it may seem difficult to understand how a subject that, for centuries, has been closely guarded within the Jewish religion, and which is deeply complicated and imbued with sacred ritual, can be the same tradition as the simple, positive-thinking, inter-faith philosophy currently being taught in books and workshops.

However, the two can live side by side very comfortably, because the secret of Kabbalah is that it is a road map to individual growth, that can be adapted for each and every individual. It can be used successfully within a religion, but it can also be used outside any conventional faith, as long as there is a belief in divinity.

Kabbalah provides a *structure* for study, growth, belief and self-realization rather than a *form*. Structure is like scaffolding: it is there to demonstrate certain simple principles of the way the universe and humanity work. But, within that scaffolding, we can grow in whatever way is right for us. The two structures that are Kabbalah's main tools for understanding are known as the Tree of Life (see right) and Jacob's Ladder (see page 8). Interpreting these gives us the ability to plot our route on our own personal life-map.

The MYSTERY traditions

The western mystery traditions include the teachings of alchemy, tarot, paganism, runes, anthroposophy, the Knights Templar, Gnosticism, Hermeticism and Rosicrucianism. These are different from the eastern mystery traditions, such as yoga and tantra, in that they are more intellectual, although these also use meditation and movement as tools.

Kabbalah exists within nearly all the western traditions as a kind of underpinning theme. Tarot, in particular, is a 'kabbalistic game', with the 22 cards of the Major Arcana representing the 22 paths on the Tree of Life; these, in turn, represent the 22 letters of the Hebrew alphabet. The four suits represent the four worlds on Jacob's Ladder. Tarot is often dismissed as a fortune-telling device, but it is a very useful tool for those who wish to understand the complexities of the 22 paths of the Tree of Life – a study that, undertaken academically, would require a thorough knowledge of the Hebrew language.

The complete western MYSTERY TRADITION

The reason why Kabbalah is known as the only 'complete' western mystery tradition is primarily because of the diagram of the Tree of Life (see right). Kabbalah teaches that this is the basis for the saying 'God made man in His own image'. This one diagram demonstrates all of human design, knowledge and experience. When the universe is described kabbalistically, it is done by repeating the same illustration viewed from four different levels – as in the diagram of Jacob's Ladder and the Four Worlds (see page 19).

The template for the designs of the Tree and the Ladder can be traced back to the Book of Exodus, and the whole of the Bible is filled with kabbalistic symbolism. Just as the Torah (the first five books of the Old Testament, and the Jewish holy books of the Law) underpins the three major western religions of

THE TREE OF LIFE

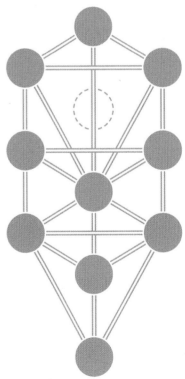

JACOB'S LADDER

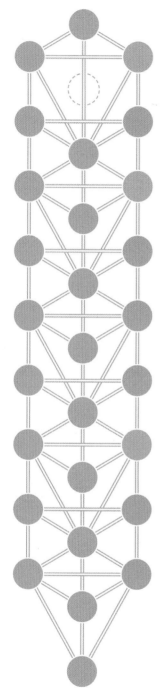

Judaism, Christianity and Islam, so Kabbalah can be described as the mystery tradition that underpins all three of those faiths. This makes it very useful for inter-faith studies and is the reason why Kabbalah is known as the Work of Unification.

The different spellings

Kabbalah is spelt in three different ways. In Hebrew it is K B L H but, as the first letter can equally be translated as a 'Q' or a 'C', different schools have used different spellings down the ages:

- ○ KABBALAH is the form generally used in Jewish, inter-faith and modern spirituality circles. It is based on Jewish tradition, with Greek and Alexandrian influences, including Platonic and Neoplatonic ones.
- ○ CABALA is the spelling normally used within esoteric Muslim and Christian circles.
- ○ QABALAH is used within the magical tradition (which peaked in the late 19th century) and in many of the other western mystery traditions that focus on tarot, alchemy, numerology and sacred geometry.

However it is spelt, the word 'Kabbalah' is Hebrew for 'receive'.

Aspects of KABBALAH

Kabbalah has two main aspects and four principal practical uses. The two main aspects are the written tradition and the oral tradition. The four principal practical uses are:

- ○ Understanding how the universe works.
- ○ Comprehending our own lives and why we are as we are.
- ○ A guide for everyday living.
- ○ A tool for interpreting religious texts such as the Bible.

All spiritual disciplines have a written tradition, which was originally intended as a guide as to what that discipline is and how to use it. However, as soon as a book or pamphlet is written, its content is crystallized and its teaching may become out of date or hard to understand as humanity evolves.

An oral tradition, on the other hand, adapts itself according to the times. This does not mean that the discipline's universal principles change, but that developments may be catered for and interpreted. The Talmud, the Jewish commentary on the Torah, began as an oral teaching as rabbis started to interpret ancient texts for more modern times.

The danger of an oral tradition is that it can be misinterpreted when its adherents do not have a sound enough understanding of the principles behind it. That is why such traditions are often kept secret: initiates are taught that they must fully understand the disciplines and the principles behind them in order to maintain balance and clarity.

Understanding how the universe works

To a kabbalist, the diagram of Jacob's Ladder is a cosmic map of how God designed and created the universe. It shows the 'invisible laws' that make life what it is and it explains the principles behind planets, angels, humanity, archetypes, animals, and good and evil. Humanity's place in the scheme of things is shown, and the four journeys that each human soul will take to reach its final goal of complete self-realization. Reincarnation is integral to kabbalistic teaching – the idea that all of us live many different lives in order to become perfected. This doctrine has always been acknowledged within the esoteric side of Judaism and Christianity, although it is still much frowned upon by the exoteric (outer) teachings.

Kabbalah also teaches the principles of cosmic law. This law is popularly known as karma, or 'what goes around comes around'. The scientist, mystic and alchemist Sir Isaac Newton defined it in his third law of motion as: 'for every action there is an equal and opposite reaction'. Kabbalistic teaching claims that this is the basis of the mathematical matrix on which our universe is designed. Some people do not like the idea of this law because they automatically assume that karma equates with 'blame', which it does not. Karma gives us back what we ourselves have given out: kindness for kindness, thoughtlessness for thoughtlessness, generosity for generosity, laughter for laughter. It is not judgemental; it is totally impartial.

Understanding our own lives

The Tree of Life, which forms a part of Jacob's Ladder, has the structural design of a human being (see page 7). No two persons' Trees will be identical – just as no two people are. Understanding the Tree can teach us where we are in balance or out of balance; whether we give too much or find it hard to receive; how we react to authority or new experiences; and how we behave in relationships. Kabbalists, just like the priests and teachers of the ancient world, use astrological principles to help explain the workings of the human psyche and the Tree of Life. The exoteric teachings of the western world do not encourage astrological knowledge because (like reincarnation) it can be

Kabbalah teaches that the universe runs on a set of principles which obey cosmic law. This 'matrix of life' applies as much to stars and galaxies as it does to humanity.

The power of Kabbalah to heal wounds that have been caused by religion should not be underestimated.

viewed as dangerous since it can so easily be manipulated or misinterpreted. However, in the 21st century both disciplines are being much more widely accepted and can now be used openly in kabbalistic teaching.

A guide for everyday living

More and more people are becoming interested in spirituality, and today there are enough groups, beliefs and sects to answer every need. But the one thing that is often missing is a 'design for living'. It is all very well to say that 'love is the answer' – and most kabbalists would agree that, ultimately, it is – but we also need to know how to pay the rent and the bills; how to deal with our in-laws and the boss; how to handle love affairs and sickness. Kabbalistic structure can help with all these concerns.

At first glance the kabbalistic diagrams look very complicated. However, after just a little study they can swiftly become a handy everyday guide to life. As they are simply a diagram of universal principles, people often demonstrate them unknowingly, whether or not they understand (or are even interested in) the esoteric. In a meeting, for example, a kabbalist might note who is sitting in which position around the table and assess his or her likely psychological profile, based on the Tree of Life. Many psychics do this intuitively, but for the kabbalist – who may not have such an ability – it is a useful tool to be able to do this intellectually.

When making plans for the day, following the structure of the Tree of Life can ensure that all the important aspects are taken care of and that balance is achieved. In undertaking a project (such as running a workshop), this will ensure that the end result is a balanced whole.

A tool for interpreting religious texts

Today most people who want to learn about Kabbalah are not religious, and they may even show resistance to the idea that kabbalistic teaching is integral to the three major religions of the western world. However, even if you have no interest in the esoteric roots of Judaism, Christianity and Islam, Kabbalah is a wonderful tool for developing self-knowledge and spirituality.

The power of Kabbalah to heal the wounds that many people feel have been caused by religion should not be underestimated. Those who have difficulty in accepting the Torah, the Bible in general, Jesus, Christianity and the New Testament have found great peace by using Kabbalah to show them the inner meanings of what may seem to be impenetrable – and often harsh – teachings.

Kabbalah is also associated with numerology, and many efforts have been made to work out hidden teachings and prophecies in the Bible, based on the numerical values of the letters of the Hebrew alphabet. But the tradition can be used far more simply than that, in identifying and translating patterns and themes in the Bible so that they are entirely relevant to the present day.

The KABBALISTIC story of creation

Because Kabbalah is associated with Judaism, its story of creation is similar to the biblical one. However, one of the reasons why it may be becoming so popular is because it begins by explaining *why* God decided to create Heaven and the Earth. The kabbalistic phrase is that 'God wished to behold God'. Modern interpretations say that God wanted to give birth.

Kabbalah teaches that each one of us is a single cell in one great, growing celestial human being named Adam Kadmon. Every one of us, whatever our race, religion or origin, is a divine spark of God's recreation of Itself. Every one of us is perfection in potential, and every one of us will return to the Source (God) as pure perfection – one day.

It takes many centuries and many lives to reach our goal. In each and every life, however, we have just one task: to be the best possible us that is feasible. Kabbalah teaches that we are not here to be Jesus Christ, Moses, Marie Curie, Mohammed, Buddha, Gandhi or Mother Teresa; we are here to be *us*. And in being *us* we will both assist in the process of creation and be happy.

KABBALISTIC history

Legend says that kabbalistic teaching dates back to the day when Adam and Eve left the Garden of Eden. The Archangel Raziel gave the first incarnated humans a 'book' that would teach them how to find their way back to Paradise. As people could rarely read and write in ancient days, this 'book' was passed down through the generations by priests and initiates via word of mouth.

Abraham and Sarah were taught by Melchizedek, King of Salem (Genesis 14: 18), at a time when the teaching had become forgotten and neglected. And most of the great Bible stories tell of initiates who brought the perennial teaching to the foreground. Moses learnt it from Jethro in the desert, before returning to Egypt to bring the Israelites out from a land that had at first been a paradise to them, but had later become a place of slavery. Other biblical initiates include Joshua, Saul, David, Solomon, Deborah, Esther and Jesus.

The Archangel Raziel escorts Adam and Eve from the Garden of Eden (Yetzirah) down into the physical world (Assiyah) where humans take on their 'coats of skin'.

Kabbalah teaches that its work is for Israelites. The term 'Israelite' means 'One who struggles with God'.

The major KABBALISTIC works

Apart from the Bible, the two most ancient and respected written guides to Kabbalah are the *Zohar* (*Book of Splendour*) and the *Sefer Yetzirah* (*Book of Formation*).

The *Zohar* is a three-volume mystical text originally thought to have been written in Israel by the Rabbi Simon Bar Yohai in the second century CE. The book was hidden for a thousand years before Rabbi Moses Ben Shem Tov de Leon of Spain published it in 1290. However, it is now thought to be more likely that Moses de Leon brought together centuries-worth of oral teachings and collated them himself, under Yohai's name, to give them greater authenticity. The *Zohar* is an account of the experiences, conversations and conclusions of a group of revered rabbis who are interpreting the Torah.

The *Sefer Yetzirah* was written sometime before the sixth century CE, but is believed to have been the work of Rabbi Akiba in around 100 CE. This book is less than 2,000 words long and focuses on the origins of the universe and humanity's place in it.

Later, the great kabbalist Moses Cordovero, who lived in Safed in Israel in the 16th century, wrote two seminal books: *Pardes Rimonim* (*The Garden of Pomegranates*), a synthesis of kabbalistic teaching, and *Tomer Devorah* (*The Palm Tree of Deborah*), which describes how we can reflect God in our daily lives.

It was Cordovero's pupil, Isaac Luria, who brought a dynamic new angle to Kabbalah, which contradicted a basic part of all prior ancient teaching. Luria taught that creation went wrong at the vital moment when God was forming the universe. The vessels (*sefirot*) that were to hold the light of creation shattered, spreading shards known as *kellipot* throughout the universe; these were the origin of evil. This teaching, known as the Lurianic tradition, took off like wildfire and became the Kabbalah that is generally known and taught today – the Kabbalah of Hasidic Jews, of the magical tradition and of the Kabbalah of the famous.

However, the old tradition – which believes that God created the world perfect and that evil comes from human misuse of free will – is now enjoying a resurgence. It is known as the Toledano tradition because it was at its peak of power and understanding in Spain during the 12th and 13th centuries.

Both traditions are valid and both work; they simply come from slightly different points on the spectrum and appeal to different kinds of people. This book acknowledges both systems but focuses on the original teachings which are simpler to understand.

Why KABBALAH is for all of us

It is said that there are 70 different forms of Kabbalah in the world – each with its own version of the esoteric teaching. Many of these have become mingled over the centuries as wise people from different traditions have discussed these among themselves.

Kabbalah teaches that its work is for *Israelites*, and not just for Jewish people. For many, the two words are synonymous, but their origins are quite different. 'Jew' means 'from the tribe of Judah' (Judah being one of the sons of Jacob) or 'from the land of Judah'. The term 'Israelite' means 'One who struggles with God'.

The biblical story of Jacob tells of his dream of a ladder ascending to Heaven, with angels ascending and descending it. In his dream, Jacob wrestles with an angel and, when their tussle has finished, the angel tells Jacob that he will be renamed Israel, because the fight has transformed him. Most people who are seeking their own individual understanding of God or of faith do the same as Jacob: they struggle with religious beliefs, concepts and dogma. The 'House of Israel' is the kabbalistic name given to those who are involved in this struggle; 'Children of Israel' are those who have not yet faced up to the fight with their concept of divinity. Israelites are both male and female; Kabbalah does not teach discrimination. Male and female are different and complementary – and both sexes contain their opposite polarity (see 'Kabbalah and relationships', pages 88–99).

The popularity of KABBALAH

Kabbalah is becoming more and more visible today because it offers a route map to spirituality that involves the idea of a Cosmic Being and a Divine Plan outside the conventional teachings of religion. People who want to understand more about themselves, and those on a spiritual path, find Kabbalah useful as a 'guidebook' to their own development and their place in the universe. Using Kabbalah, we can learn to understand our physical make-up and why some parts of us are stronger than others. We can also comprehend the relationship between our physical, mental and emotional responses. The sefirot (spheres) on the Tree of Life (see page 15) correspond to the human body and the human psyche. They show our levels of personality, soul and spirit, and they can help us to make sense of an increasingly confusing world and find balance where before there was only confusion.

Jacob's dream, showing angels ascending and descending a heavenly ladder through the worlds of Earth, Water, Air and Fire.

The
DIAGRAMS

Kabbalah was originally a purely oral tradition. However, any oral teaching can become like 'Chinese whispers' if it does not have an underlying structure to help people know whether the teaching they are receiving is accurate.

THE MENORAH

- NEZACH
- HESED
- HOKHMAH
- KETER
- BINAH
- GEVURAH
- HOD
- DA'AT
- TIFERET
- YESOD
- MALKHUT

In Exodus (25–7) it is taught that God gave the original designs for the Tree of Life and Jacob's Ladder to Moses at the time of the exodus from Egypt, so that the Israelites would have a 'living tradition' to help them through the years in the wilderness. The original kabbalistic structure was a seven-branched candlestick made of pure gold. It was known as the Menorah (see left) and was smelted from the treasure that the Israelites took from Egypt. The Menorah and the Ark of the Covenant (the sacred box where the Ten Commandments were kept) stood in the Tabernacle that the Israelites built as their movable temple in the wilderness.

Moses was given direct instructions as to how both the Menorah and the Tabernacle should be built. They were designed so that initiates from those times could understand the whole of the teaching by reference to the markings on the Menorah and the design of the Tabernacle. Solomon's Temple in Jerusalem was also built to the same design.

The kabbalistic diagrams of the Tree of Life and Jacob's Ladder are all adapted from these original biblical instructions. They were formulated in the early 13th century by the school of Isaac the Blind in Gerona, Spain. Isaac lived in Narbonne, France, between 1165 and 1235, and it is thought that his Gerona school developed as a response to the rationalist philosophy of the school of Maimonides (1135–1204) in Cordoba. Maimonides was a great scholar and teacher who linked the Jewish tradition to Aristotelian doctrine whereas Isaac the Blind and his school veered towards the more mystical line taken by the Greek philosopher Plato and by the Neoplatonism that followed him. Knowledge of Jacob's Ladder was actually 'hidden' for four centuries and only re-emerged in the public domain in the 1970s.

At first sight the diagrams look complicated. However, understanding them is rather like learning a foreign language and eventually it becomes second nature. Every time you work with the Tree you are working with your own spiritual blueprint, so it is always a journey of self-discovery.

The TREE OF LIFE

The Tree of Life is a blueprint of a perfect human being. It is mostly used to represent our psychological being, although it can also be used to show our physical body. It is a diagram of someone who is looking away from us. The Bible and the oral teaching say that God does not reveal his face to us while we are incarnate, for the brightness would destroy us. The right hand of the Tree represents our right-hand side and the left-hand side, our left. The central column is our psychological backbone.

The Tree is an extraordinary thing. If you ask someone to draw it freehand, the picture they create will give the kabbalist a perfect diagnostic tool with which to establish where their life is in or out of balance at that particular moment.

Kabbalah teaches that the Tree of Life was formed by God in a zigzag known as the Lightning Flash (see right) to ensure that the energies of the right and left sides balanced out. Ten circular vessels known as sefirot (Hebrew for 'sphere' or 'sapphire') represent the ten aspects that kabbalists believe are the Divine Image of God – and, therefore, images of us too. An 11th sefirah (sefirah is the singular of sefirot), called Da'at, looks like a black hole and can either transmit knowledge between levels or act as a kind of plughole to drain ideas away, when they are not strong enough to thrive.

The 11 sefirot are known as:

○ MALKHUT: the Kingdom; the place of physical reality and the fulfilment of plans
○ YESOD: the Foundation; the place of the human ego, and the persona or 'mask' that we wear in public

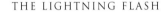

THE LIGHTNING FLASH

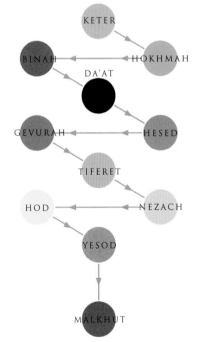

THE SEFIROT

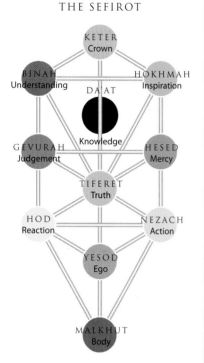

- ○ HOD: Reverberation; the place of information and communication
- ○ NEZACH: Eternity; the place of impulse and sexuality
- ○ TIFERET: Beauty; the place of the true self
- ○ GEVURAH: Judgement; the place of discipline and discernment
- ○ HESED: Loving Kindness; the place of unconditional love and mercy
- ○ DA'AT: Knowledge; the window between worlds
- ○ BINAH: Understanding; the place where experience, knowledge and information merge
- ○ HOKHMAH: Wisdom or Revelation; the place of inspiration
- ○ KETER: The Crown; the link with God

The TREE as a boat

A good way to look at the Tree of Life design for the first time is to view it as a boat, with Tiferet as the boatman. If we sit in the centre of the boat looking forward to Keter, we are balanced; if we sit too far forward or back, or too far to left or right, then we are likely to make the boat wobble or even capsize.

In front of the captain's seat of Tiferet is Da'at, the black hole. This is also called the 'window between worlds', and to look through it we need to be firmly placed in Tiferet. If we are not balanced, this can feel like taking out the bung in the bottom of the boat and letting the water rush in.

At the prow is Keter, the Crown. From Keter we can see and even touch the Divine, but we cannot spend all our time there because we would lose any sense of reality and tip the boat too far forward.

Behind us, in the boat, is Yesod, the Foundation. This is the place of the ego – the servant of the self – and is where the captain's second-in-command would sit in the boat. In fact, he or she would be the one doing most of the day-to-day work, while the captain looks ahead and observes what is going on. Yesod's job is to handle the everyday affairs of our life, such as driving the car, preparing our meals and choosing what to wear.

If Yesod takes over charge of the boat instead of the captain at Tiferet, then the boat will tip up just enough to block our view of where we should be heading. This is exactly what the human ego does when it is undisciplined. Kabbalistic work is about ensuring that Yesod acts as a foundation for Tiferet, so that we can live consciously instead of running on automatic all the time.

Behind Yesod in the stern is Malkhut, the Kingdom – our physical body and its desires. Just like Keter, Malkhut is a vital part of our life, but too much time spent focusing on the physical has just as negative an effect as constantly living in the clouds, and can tip the boat up.

The SEVEN LEVELS

There are seven different levels in the Tree of Life. Nowadays they are shown in the same colours as the chakras (energy centres) of Hindu tradition, which are used in many healing therapies around the world. The seven levels of the Tree and the chakras represent the same aspects of the body and the psyche – showing the way that esoteric traditions hold the same truths (see right):

○ MALKHUT: red – the Base Chakra; physical life

○ HOD-NEZACH-YESDOD: orange – the Gonadic Chakra; sexuality and the ego

○ HOD-TIFERET-NEZACH: yellow – the Solar Plexus Chakra; the true self

○ HOD-GEVURAH-TIFERET and TIFERET-HESED-NEZACH: green – the Heart Chakra; the level of love

○ BINAH-HOKHMAH-TIFERET: blue – the Throat Chakra; the level of communication and psychic awareness

○ BINAH-TIFERET-GEVURAH and HOKHMAH-HESED-TIFERET: purple – the Brow Chakra or Third Eye; the level of intuition

○ BINAH-KETER-HOKHMAH: white – the Crown Chakra; the place of the higher self and contact with God

The THREE PILLARS

There are three vertical pillars on the Tree (see page 18). The right-hand one is the masculine, active pillar and the left-hand one is the feminine, passive pillar. The central one is the pillar of consciousness; it holds the balance between giving and receiving, action and passivity, positivity and negativity, light and dark, day and night.

In kabbalistic teaching 'masculine' does not mean 'of a man' and 'feminine' does not mean 'of a woman'. Both sexes carry masculine and feminine traits within them. Somebody who is born male may have a very strong feminine side; likewise, a woman may have a very strong masculine side. We live in a world of duality, and because day is more obvious than night and positive is more exciting than negative, people often mistake one side as being more powerful than the other. But the left-hand, feminine side of the Tree of Life and the right-hand, masculine side are as strong and important as each other.

The left-hand pillar is the part of us that receives information and knowledge, thinks things through and makes decisions based on our level of understanding. Martial arts, rather surprisingly, are an example of the feminine – they use controlled, flowing movements and, when the need arises, employ the weight and strength of an opponent to overcome them.

THE CHAKRAS

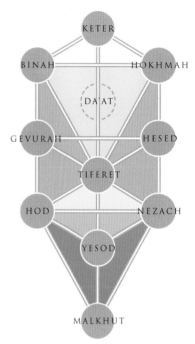

□ CROWN CHAKRA
▨ BROW CHAKRA
▢ THROAT CHAKRA
▨ HEART CHAKRA
▢ SOLAR PLEXUS CHAKRA
▨ GONADIC CHAKRA
■ BASE CHAKRA

THE THREE PILLARS

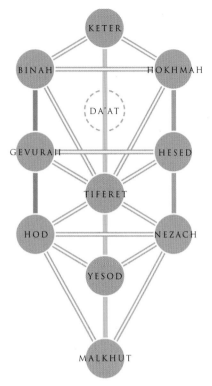

■ PASSIVE PRINCIPLE
■ COLUMN OF CONSCIOUSNESS
■ ACTIVE PRINCIPLE

The right-hand pillar is the part of us that acts on inspiration, that gives and generally achieves things. Each pillar is out of balance without the other.

The sefirot on each of the two side columns also need each other for balance. At the top, Hokhmah (Revelation) needs Binah (Understanding) – or a great idea just becomes a flash-in-the-pan. Hesed (Loving Kindness) needs Gevurah (Judgement) or it will give too much and exhaust itself. Nezach (usually translated as Eternity, but for these purposes best called Action) needs Hod (Reverberation, better translated as Reaction) in order to work.

You can see how this works by thinking of a good idea and following it down the Tree on the Lightning Flash (see page 15), from first inspiration to the fulfilment of your wish. For example, the idea of running a workshop on your chosen subject might go like this:

○ KETER 'Oh! I've got an idea!'
○ HOKHMAH 'I could do a workshop!'
○ BINAH 'Do I understand enough about the subject – and how to run a workshop?'
○ (At this point the idea either takes root or falls away into the black hole at Da'at.)
○ HESED 'I'd love to do that. I will do it! It will help other people too.'
○ GEVURAH 'I must find time and organize myself properly. Am I really brave enough to do this? Am I sure I know enough?'
○ TIFERET 'This feels really right. I know I can do it.'
○ NEZACH 'I must start to organize, write leaflets, find a place to hold the workshop.'
○ HOD 'I mustn't be discouraged by all the effort required. I must go over it all again to make sure it's accurate and that it will work.'
○ YESOD 'How do I make it attractive to people so that they will want to come? Am I sure this isn't just an ego trip for me?'
○ MALKHUT 'It's ready to roll!'

The top sefirot often appear to be the most exciting ones, with all the inspiration and ideas, while the lower ones represent the hard work that is needed to make things happen. Too much enthusiasm (at Hokhmah, Hesed and Nezach) or too much criticism (at Binah, Gevurah and Hod) can over-balance the whole project.

In Kabbalah we are taught that the way to create unity within ourselves is to stand firm on the central pillar of the Tree of Life, holding on to the two side pillars and thereby balancing them out. It is all about learning to be conscious of who we really are.

JACOB'S LADDER and the four worlds

Jacob's Ladder (see page 8) is a diagram of the universe. It contains four versions of the Tree of Life, each of which represents a different world: the physical, psychological, spiritual and divine worlds. The four worlds also represent the four elements of Earth, Water, Air and Fire. The fifth element from Chinese philosophy, usually referred to as Metal, would be a fusion of the upper and lower worlds (Earth and Fire) and is sometimes referred to as the Fifth Great Tree, which runs straight up the central pillar.

The kabbalistic story of creation tells of how God, being absolute, had to withdraw in order to create a space (or a womb) of nothingness into which he could breathe the essence of creation. Jacob's Ladder was the result of this breath; the first world, known as AZILUT, is the divine template of a great being known as Adam Kadmon – a blueprint of a perfected human being. The 'molecules' that make up Adam Kadmon (who has no gender) are the essence of what will become individual human beings when they descend through the lower worlds (see below).

Kabbalah teaches that each of us comes from one aspect of Adam Kadmon and has a particular destiny to fulfil – whether this is to be the perfect soldier, philosopher, lover, teacher, or whatever. Kabbalistic sources disagree on whether our souls have a specific gender, but those who say they do not still agree that each soul has a tendency to incarnate as one sex or the other, according to its particular destiny.

From Azilut, this world of the divine human being, flowed BERIAH, the spiritual world. This is the realm of creation and ideas, so you could say that Azilut was the spark and Beriah the concept. Neither world has any form or image, so they are hard to imagine and even harder to describe. Neither operates in time as we understand it, either. It is said that all that has happened, and all that will happen, is already recorded in these two worlds. At the Beriatic level, the right-hand side of the Ladder is pure creation and the left-hand side is pure destruction – both characteristics being as important as the other, and just as dangerous if misused.

As the light flows down the Ladder, further into the void/womb and further from its Source, its quality coarsens. Azilut is Fire, Beriah is Air, and the third world, YEZIRAH, is the world of Water. This is the world where time begins; the one where forms exist and definitions can be made. For instance, the idea of a dog comes from Beriah, but the different types of dog (basset hound, poodle, and so on) are defined in Yezirah. This is also the world of mental

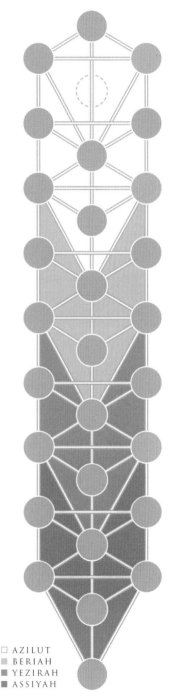

THE FOUR WORLDS

☐ AZILUT
▨ BERIAH
■ YEZIRAH
■ ASSIYAH

images, emotion and the human soul. Paradise is in Yezirah and so is Hell; they are both psychological realities, and Kabbalah teaches that we can live in either of them in our minds at any time, whether we are alive or dead.

Finally there is ASSIYAH, the world of Earth, where we are physically incarnated to play the great Game of Life. Although the lowest world appears to us to be very strong, it is the most fragile of the four. The physical Earth could be destroyed very easily but the Yeziratic, Beriatic and Azilutic Earths would still exist. All great spiritual traditions teach that it is only our physical bodies that die, while our souls go on.

In this great kabbalistic scheme of life, humans are the only beings who have access to all four worlds of Jacob's Ladder. Archangels have access only to the top two; angels only to the middle two; and animals only to the bottom two. We humans are made in the image of God and our job is to reflect all that is in creation back to the Source. As we grow, so the divine baby grows. Kabbalah teaches that we are still very young and that we are not doing quite as badly as some of us fear.

The FOUR JOURNEYS

Kabbalah teaches that our life takes us on four major journeys:

- ○ THE FIRST DESCENT: we come down from the heavens into the physical world once our souls have been called forth (Azilut), created (Beriah), formed (Yezirah) and made (Assiyah).
- ○ THE FIRST ASCENT: once we have fully incarnated, we climb back up through the worlds towards God, learning how to exist on Earth, how to make a living, universal principles, love and discernment.
- ○ THE SECOND DESCENT: once we have learnt techniques for living happily, we descend again to teach and help out our fellow humans who have not yet learnt what we know.
- ○ THE SECOND ASCENT: the fourth journey is the final return to the Light as completed, fulfilled human beings.

Journeys two and three are often carried out simultaneously – learning a little and teaching it in one life, then learning a little more. These two journeys are depicted in the ancient Hindu mystical game known as Moskha Patamu (now called Snakes and Ladders); we climb and fall as we learn or make mistakes.

Kabbalists believe that it would not be fair, or possible, for a human soul to reach enlightenment in just one life. Even the greatest souls are believed to have lived many lives before incarnating as astonishing beings who have changed the world.

Exercise
Drawing your Tree of Life

Hand-drawing the Tree of Life is a powerful exercise that enables you to establish where you are out of balance in your sefirot.

Copy the diagrams of the Tree (see right). Keep it simple: draw the sefirot and the paths freehand. The interpretations that follow are very basic, but you will soon learn how to understand your own Tree. Remember that the image you are drawing is only representative of you now, and it may change as your feelings alter over the hours, weeks and months to come. Looking at the diagram you have drawn, note the following:

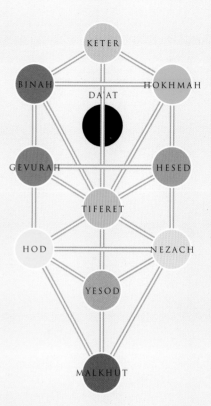

- ○ If any of the sefirot are considerably larger or smaller than the others, then you are particularly strong or weak in that area. The same goes with the triads (the triangular areas between the sefirot).
- ○ If any of the sefirot have open gaps, or if any of the paths break into the sefirot, you may have a weakness in your physical or psychological boundaries in that area.
- ○ If any of the paths are very wide, narrow or broken, the sefirot that are linked by them may have trouble communicating with each other.
- ○ If you forget to fill in any of the paths, then that part of your psyche is quite unformed and would benefit from some attention.
- ○ If your left-hand sefirot are larger than your right-hand ones, you have a tendency to be over-passive, over-critical, over-studious or over-judgemental.
- ○ If your right-hand sefirot are larger than your left-hand ones, you have a tendency to be over-active, over-generous, over-sensitive or wildly unpredictable.

A powerful exercise to heal any imbalances that your diagram shows in your psychological Tree of Life is to paint the Tree exactly, using a ruler and compass (see page 122). This helps you focus on the balance you would like to achieve and can have amazing results in healing.

MAKING THE TREE WITH THE BODY

KETER

BINAH

HOKHMAH

DA'AT

GEVURAH

HESED

TIFERET

HOD

NEZACH

YESOD

MALKHUT

Exercise

Making the Tree with your body

A good way to understand the Tree of Life is to create the sefirot with your body as an active meditation. In this exercise you go up the Tree and then down again, experiencing each sefirah both physically and emotionally.

Going up the Tree

○ MALKHUT **Stand with your legs apart, leaning as far down as you can.** Sense the physical weight of your body and the power of the life-force within you. Imagine a cord extending from your feet to the centre of the Earth, grounding and strengthening you.

○ YESOD **Stand upright with your legs apart, with your hands on your lower stomach.** Sense the power of the sexuality within you; feel the everyday stresses and strains, the anger and grief that you often experience as you go through life. Think about how you enjoyed your last visit to the cinema or going out with friends. Consider your position in life, your work and your family – and how quickly your moods can change as you are loved or challenged by others.

○ HOD **Stand upright, leaning slightly to the left, with your left arm slightly raised.** Do you feel a bit unbalanced on this side of the Tree? Think about the books you like to read; about your favourite way of communicating with others: by telephone? email? letter? text? Think about the tasks that you do every day of your life, again and again, such as washing, dressing, driving and working.

○ NEZACH **Stand upright, leaning slightly to the right with your right arm slightly raised.** Do you feel balanced or unbalanced on this side of the Tree? Think about the changes you have made in your life over the years and the impulses that caused them. Consider how you dress to make yourself attractive to others. Reflect on the people you find sexually attractive. Think about what art you find beautiful.

○ TIFERET **Stand upright with your hands on your solar plexus (the part of your stomach beneath your diaphragm).** Think about who you really are, as opposed to all the opinions, flattery or criticism of others. Seek a stillness and peace inside you by clearing your mind of memory and anticipation – even if only for a few seconds. Stand tall, relax your body and know that you are powerful and strong.

○ GEVURAH **Stand upright, leaning slightly to the left, with your left arm extended at shoulder height.** Think about how hard it is to keep that arm steady for a long time. Consider how hard or easy you find it to make decisions. Are you able to say 'No' comfortably when you don't want to do what others want you to? Are you clear about the path you want to take in the next months and years of your life?

○ HESED **Stand upright, leaning slightly to the right, with your right arm extended at shoulder height.** Think about the idea of unconditional love – allowing others to be what they want to be without interfering; forgiving those who have hurt you; looking after those who need your care.

○ DA'AT **Stand upright with both hands in front of your eyes.** Close your eyes. Feel the difference that darkness makes in your psyche. Are you afraid of the dark or does it excite you? Can you shift levels for a moment and experience another reality – another world?

○ BINAH **Open your eyes and stand upright, leaning slightly to the left, with your left arm raised diagonally.** Think about the times when you have transformed information into knowledge; how you 'just know' how to carry out your work or be a parent. Consider what you 'know' about divinity and your place in life.

○ HOKHMAH **Stand upright, leaning slightly to the right, with your right arm raised diagonally.** Open your eyes wide and think about inspiration, revelation and the times when you have suddenly had a brilliant idea or an inspirational thought.

○ KETER **Stand upright with both hands raised above your head, looking upwards.** Feel your link to the Divine above and your link to the Earth below your feet. You may even feel a rush of energy coming into your body from top to toe.

Coming down the Tree

○ To come down the Tree, you reverse the entire process, starting at KETER and finishing at MALKHUT, where you bend down towards the Earth, relaxing your body as much as you can and transmitting the divine energy and knowledge right down through your body and into the centre of the Earth.

○ By doing this exercise you can see how life looks very different when approached with the thoughts and feelings you experience in the lower sefirot compared with how it is when you are in touch with your higher self. It is easy to get bogged down in everyday life and troubles, but if you can take a wider view, problems can be clarified and eased.

○ Quite often, doing this exercise with a specific problem in mind – and looking at it from the point of view of each sefirah – will help you to find a clear and appropriate answer by the time you have come back down the Tree.

Practical uses of
KABBALAH

Kabbalah works on the principle that there are ten aspects to God and, because we are all made in God's image, the same ten aspects apply to every human being. Unless all ten aspects are aligned, our lives will not be as harmonious as they could be.

Playing the GAME OF LIFE

The 'Game of Life' for the kabbalist is to work out these ten aspects of ourselves and how they relate to each other. We can then balance and heal them consciously through knowledge, meditation and action.

Each of the four worlds of Jacob's Ladder (see right) is linked to the other worlds, and Kabbalah teaches that action, thought or feeling vibrates into these other worlds. This principle can be seen in both conventional and complementary healing. A doctor may prescribe a drug for a physical complaint (in Assiyah, the world of Earth), which eases pain or congestion and also makes the patient feel better psychologically (in Yezirah). The drug and its effects may dissolve the problem on one level and their healing may vibrate through to another level.

However, practitioners of complementary medicine believe that to treat the symptom of a disease in Assiyah is not enough. The *cause* of the physical complaint needs to be addressed too, and this cause will generally come from our thoughts and feelings in Yezirah. Many complementary therapies (such as homeopathy and spiritual healing) are 'unprovable' by science because they are intended to work in Yezirah – or even in Beriah – with their effects vibrating through to Assiyah.

The kabbalistic Game is to find our 'real selves': the Tiferet point on the Tree of Life (see page 15). At that point we can be awake to our strengths and our limitations, and can decide what needs to be celebrated and enjoyed – and what might need a little work. If you look at the four worlds of Jacob's Ladder (see right), you will notice that the Tiferet of Yezirah is also the Keter of Assiyah and the Malkut of Beriah.

This means that someone who is 'centred' is aware of the whole of the physical world beneath and is connected to the spiritual world above. Just as the word Malkhut means 'Kingdom' and Beriah means both 'Spirit' and 'Heaven' (see page 15), so, at Tiferet, we are in the place known in the Bible as the Kingdom of Heaven: a place of perfect balance where we can see clearly all around us. With that awareness, and with plenty of practice, a kabbalist can understand what it feels like to be so balanced, and can consciously move his or her self to that place by an act of will, even in times of crisis.

From Tiferet, it is possible to raise our consciousness up to the Keter of Yezirah (which is also the Malkhut of Azilut, the kingdom of the divine world). Kabbalah teaches that this psychological place, where we have direct contact with divinity, is what Jesus of Nazareth was referring to when he spoke of the 'Kingdom of God.'

When the GAME is no game

For some people the idea of life being a game is difficult to handle. Life can be very hard and particular situations almost unbearable. For instance, persecution, abuse, sickness and pain are not things to be treated lightly.

Kabbalah teaches that we are all dealt a particular hand of cards in each lifetime. Some of us have far more challenges to face than others; some of us even have a genetic make-up that will result in sickness and maybe even early death. The idea of a law of cause and effect can be frightening, because it appears to imply that our thoughts and actions can bring terrible diseases and crises upon us. Some people think that kabbalists and others who believe in reincarnation are imposing blame on the innocent by believing in the law of karma.

There is nothing in kabbalistic teaching that imputes blame. It is generally believed among modern kabbalists who have experience of the higher worlds that human beings have a measure of choice in their decisions about incarnation. As Kabbalah teaches that all human beings are seeking to perfect

THE FOUR WORLDS

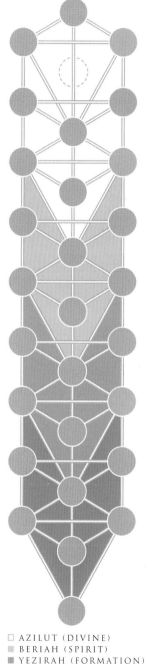

☐ AZILUT (DIVINE)
▨ BERIAH (SPIRIT)
▩ YEZIRAH (FORMATION)
■ ASSIYAH (PHYSICAL)

For the kabbalist, the task is to consciously lift ourselves up so that we can practise free will and live life as fully as possible.

themselves over many lifetimes, it is likely that each one of us will, at some point, choose lives that others may view as difficult, so that we can experience all that Earth has to offer and understand everything there is to learn.

Kabbalistically, this would not be seen as any different from someone such as Mother Teresa choosing to live her life in extreme poverty in order to help others, when she could easily have become a wealthy media personality and author, describing her early experiences in Calcutta. It is inconceivable that she would have done so – just as it is inconceivable to some souls that they should turn their backs on a particularly challenging life that they have chosen.

The most important element here is the concept of free will. Kabbalah teaches that free will can only be practised from the level of Tiferet and above. Sometimes a person who is able to be at Tiferet can even remember why they chose a particular life. Once that memory is accessed, it usually brings great peace and contentment with the chosen path – no matter how hard that life may seem to others.

Below Tiferet, in everyday life, we are all subject to the karma of the country in which we live, the genetic structure into which we are born and the social world around us. For the kabbalist, the task is to consciously lift ourselves up so that we can practise free will and live life as fully as possible.

How to play the GAME to win

Knowledge of the rules is the first step in playing to win. Here are the basic rules, as understood by the modern kabbalist:

You have been given the tools you need to make your life happy within the available parameters. These tools are unique to you. The rule book describing how the universe works is available to you within the belief system (if any) of your birth, and in any other belief system that you choose. You may have to look into the heart of that system if you have chosen a particularly challenging life, because the exoteric (outer) system may not be clear enough for you.

Although Kabbalah pre-dates the written Torah, the rules of life for those born into the Jewish or Christian tradition are all present in the Bible. This is why Kabbalah can be such a powerful tool in assisting inter-faith studies and in healing the hurts that people may have experienced through conventional Judaism and Christianity.

The rules of the universe are the laws of cause and effect or, as they are termed nowadays, 'What goes around, comes around'. To the kabbalist, however, the way to apply these laws is best laid out in the Ten Commandments, each of which represents one of the ten sefirot of the Tree of Life (see page 15).

Kabbalah teaches that the original Ten Commandments, which Moses threw down and destroyed when he saw the Israelites worshipping the Golden Calf, were carved by light in sapphire (the Hebrew root of S P H R for 'sefirah' is the same as that for 'sapphire'). They carried an esoteric version of the law, which was much lighter than the later version outlined in the Bible, in that it formed 'guides for living', rather than commandments.

With their 'graven in stone' and 'secrets of light' aspects, every one of the Ten Commandments is a lesson in keeping the One Great Law that supersedes all others – the law of cause and effect. If we obey that law, everything else falls into place, and we become masters of our destiny. It is all in the interpretation. A kabbalist – just like any other person who wants to follow the spirit rather than the *letter* of the law – will weigh each one of the Ten Commandments and make a decision, both according to the law and with relevance to the situation at hand (see page 67).

The NEW AGE and RELIGION

Kabbalah provides a vital link between New Age beliefs and conventional religion. For many, Kabbalah is thought to be a New Age fad with no connection to 'serious' teaching at all. However, its seminal books (the *Zohar, Sefer Yetzirah* and *Pardes Rimonim*) are respected historical documents providing valuable commentaries on the Jewish Torah.

Orthodox Jewish kabbalists have been known to object to the teaching of Kabbalah to those outside the Jewish faith, stating that it cannot be understood or practised without a deep study of the commentaries and rituals within orthodox Jewry. It is true that Kabbalah is best understood with reference to the Torah – in fact, this is a wonderful key to understanding all aspects of the Bible. But Kabbalah can also be used as a structure for living outside conventional religion.

If you take the inner teachings of Judaism out of Kabbalah, you lose its foundation – the two all-important diagrams of the Tree of Life and Jacob's Ladder. Kabbalah's link to the esoteric teachings of the Bible is its strength and explains why it can help to heal the wounds between different faiths.

By its links to conventional religion and its acceptance of practices and beliefs such as the effects of the planets on our lives, reincarnation and the power of the mind, Kabbalah demonstrates that New Age philosophies are also old and practical doctrines used by spiritual leaders such as Moses and Jesus of Nazareth.

Every one of the Ten Commandments is a lesson in keeping the One Great Law that supersedes all others – the law of cause and effect.

THE PLANETS

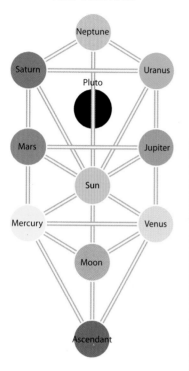

People sometimes object to the idea that such practices could ever have been linked to religious faith, but historical research provides good evidence that it is so. Evidence of the use of astrology, for example, can be seen in a 1st-century mosaic on the floor of a synagogue in Tiberius, Israel; in the astrological calendar in the medieval cathedral of Bologna, Italy; and in the zodiac window and astrological clock in the great cathedral of Chartres, France. In ancient days the movements of the planets were used to assist the planting of crops, the planning of great events and to teach archetypical legends, because people were unaware of their time and date of birth. Astrology has become far more refined over the years, but, as Kabbalah is also a living tradition, they have been able to evolve together.

Today astrology is seen as an integral part of Kabbalah and as a useful tool for understanding the Tree of Life. Plotting your birth chart onto the Tree (see page 55) can help you perceive your life path and destiny with much greater ease than was possible in earlier times. To do this, put the sign of your Ascendant at Malkhut, your Moon at Yesod, your Mercury at Hod, your Venus at Nezach, your Sun at Tiferet, your Mars at Gevurah, your Jupiter at Hesed, your Pluto at Da'at, your Saturn at Binah, your Uranus at Hokhmah and your Neptune at Keter. We will look more closely at astrology in Chapter 5.

It is fair to say that many so-called New Age beliefs (including astrology and spiritual healing) were frowned upon in the past, unless they were practised by people with great knowledge and learning. This is no different from the desire to ensure that doctors and practitioners of any therapy are licensed and can prove they have done the necessary training to carry out their craft properly. A little learning can be a dangerous thing, especially when dealing with the human soul.

GOD and gender

One of the uses of Kabbalah in helping to make peace between religion and the New Age concerns the gender of God. In Judaism, Islam and Christianity, God is referred to as 'He' – the idea of the Great Father. In paganism and some New Age teaching, God is better known as 'the Goddess' and is thought to be feminine.

Judaism forbade the making of images of God, but Christian painters have often depicted God as an old man watching us from the sky, which has reinforced the belief in the masculinity of the Divine. The idea of 'God the Father, God the Son and God the Holy Spirit' adds to this.

Kabbalah teaches two main points about the gender of God:

○ The supernal (celestial) triad (Binah/Keter/Hokhmah) represents divinity.
○ Keter (the Crown or the One) is the place of unity with Hokhmah as the masculine principle and Binah as the feminine principle.

The traditional image of 'God the Father.' Kabbalah teaches that God is neither masculine nor feminine.

The implication is that God has both masculine and feminine elements and that the two combine to become the One. This One has no gender whatsoever.

An alternative kabbalistic view is that Keter represents God the Father (the giving principle), with Malkhut representing God the Mother (the receiving principle). As no process in creation is complete without both Keter and Malkhut, kabbalists believe that once the Tree is 'realized' – that is, once we are in balance with all aspects of the Tree within ourselves – all the way from the top to the bottom, a sacred marriage occurs between the masculine and feminine, again creating the One: Unity. Therefore the kabbalist's answer to the question 'Is God male or female?' is: 'Neither'.

It can be useful to refer to God as 'It' rather than 'He' or 'She', both to demonstrate the idea of Unity and to help people realize how much they may project onto the idea of God the Father or the Mother Goddess. Such projections sometimes inhibit spiritual growth because they make it harder to open the mind to new concepts.

Understanding the EGO and the SELF

Kabbalah teaches that the ego is our foundation. Its role is to take care of everyday life and support our self. The self is that part of us which lives life consciously and searches for spiritual growth. Ego is about reaction: the re-acting of the same thing over and over again. Self is about response: from the New Testament Greek *re-spondo*, meaning to think again, or to consider new possibilities.

Scientists now know that the human mind needs us to repeat new tasks many times before we are comfortable with them, because the brain needs to make the activity automatic. To the kabbalist, this is the essence of Tiferet and Yesod. Any brand-new situation in our lives – a crisis or an amazing opportunity – may leave us temporarily at a loss because our Yesod (our Foundation, see page 15) does not know how to respond. In Kabbalah such a situation is known as 'the wake-up call'. Then some inner strength or ability from Tiferet (Beauty, the place of the true self) may manifest within us; we think differently for a while, instead of following old habits. However, once we are used to a situation, we are likely to go back to running on automatic.

The main purpose of meditation is to still Yesod and contact Tiferet so that we can get new insights into our lives.

When there is such a crisis or opportunity, Yesod can act as our true foundation; it keeps us functioning normally – going to work, doing everyday tasks – while Tiferet deals with the situation at hand. Yesod also offers memory and similar past experiences to help Tiferet make the all-important decisions that are necessary. If Yesod is out of balance, it may resist (and even fight) new impulses from Tiferet in order not to change the status quo.

The main purpose of meditation is to still Yesod and contact Tiferet so that we can get new insights into our lives, instead of thinking the same thoughts again and again or resisting anything new.

Kabbalists say that if a situation arises that upsets or angers us, we have only a few seconds to access Tiferet and see the truth of the matter before Yesod kicks in. Ego is automatic and, if the situation has happened before, Yesod's reaction will be the same as it was the previous time and the chance to resolve the situation may have been lost.

Modern kabbalists often use astrology to help them assess the characteristics of all the sefirot. This is useful in working out when we are coming from Yesod and when we are coming from Tiferet. Astrology belongs only to the Yeziratic world (see page 19) and it can be helpful to regard it as a language, rather than a science or an art. Like Kabbalah, astrology interprets a human being's 'blueprint' for life and shows exactly what that person is and will be – if he or she does not use free will and make deliberate choices. Both astrologers and kabbalists agree that conscious choice can, and will, overrule astrology.

Many people say, 'I'm not at all like my Sun sign' and they are probably right. The reason for that is that the Sun sign is Tiferet (see page 28), while most of us live the majority of our lives in our Moon sign (Yesod).

The difference between SPIRITUALITY and MAGIC

Kabbalah has occasionally got itself a bad name over the centuries because it can be successfully used for magic. And magic has always been a much-misunderstood concept. The goal of the kabbalist is to learn to develop his or her talents and skills and use them to create balance and to help further the work of God on Earth. To the kabbalist, there is a clear distinction between 'black magic' and 'white magic', although *all* magic is about manipulating the world of Yezirah to create what the human will desires. Black magic involves manipulating the world of forms to cause harm to others; white magic means doing the same to create good for others or ourselves.

However, a kabbalist is taught that none of us on Earth can know what is the highest good for ourselves or others. We may want the love of a particular man or woman, but it may not be our destiny or something that will, ultimately, bring us joy. To use magic to draw that person to us is seen as incorrect and may be dangerous – it could even block the arrival of our true love, who is being hidden by our current desire.

Many people who call themselves witches are working for the highest good of all and 'cast spells' solely to draw people's natural good to them – this is what a kabbalist would call spirituality, and not magic. In magic the human will is used to create 'my will' (see page 48); in spirituality it is used to dissolve the blocks within us that prevent God's will from manifesting in our lives.

It can be hard to understand that God's will is the best thing for us, for our religious upbringing often teaches us fear of God. But through Kabbalah – and particularly by using biblical teachings – we can come to understand that the will of the Holy One for us is always (and only) good and happiness. This does not mean that we will not face challenges and tragedies in life, but that the support and help we need will always be there for us.

No one who truly understands cosmic law is likely to want to practise magic. If you use magic to impose your will on someone else, then magic will be used on you, multiplied many times. There is likely to be a karmic backlash, a bit like the snap-back of a rubber band used as a catapult. However, there is an instant way to transform magic into spirituality – just add the words 'If it be Thy Will'. It is important to be aware that if your wish is not in accordance with Divine Order, nothing will happen.

Down the ages, magic has generally been used to get people what they want *now* – as a kind of mystical credit card. It is interesting to question whether, if we had to save for a year or more in order to buy that new car or hi-fi, we would actually want that particular brand by the time we had the cash.

The New Age practice of affirmation is sometimes seen as being magical. An affirmation is the repetition of positive phrases in the present tense to reprogramme the psyche from old and unhelpful patterns. However, if an affirmation is used as a tool for changing the self, then it becomes spirituality. Louise L. Hay, author of the bestselling book *You Can Heal Your Life*, recommends using the phrase 'I approve of myself' as the foundation of all affirmation work. Done consciously, this affirmation moves us from our Yesodic habit-thinking into Tiferet. It usually feels quite untrue when we begin to repeat it, but that very repetition acts as a 'computer reprogrammer' on Yesod, so that it comes to believe that it is true.

Ancient societies developed profound knowledge of how the Universe works by simple observation of the movement of the Earth and the stars.

The inner voices that nag at us that an affirmation is wrong – and which berate us for even daring to think we are worthy of approval – come from many hidden aspects with the Tree, not just Yesod. Wherever they come from, with patience they can be outpaced, because they are only old programmes and thoughts running on automatic.

Understanding how the UNIVERSE works

Kabbalah teaches that the process of creation is a result of God wishing to behold God. In other words, God is reproducing Itself. This 'cosmic baby' is made up of the spirits and souls of everything in existence, from an amoeba to an angel. Human beings are said to be made in the image of God, and each one of us is a vital aspect in this process of evolution. A kabbalist is taught that we each represent God on Earth, and that God observes creation through our eyes.

We have many lives to live in order to learn how the universe works. Many mystics believe that it takes dozens – even hundreds – of lives to build the foundation (Yesod) just to know how to feed and support ourselves properly. We are always in contact with the higher worlds, if we are open to the idea – no matter what kind of life we are living (simple or sophisticated). So-called 'primitive societies' often have profound spiritual beliefs based on observation of the Earth and the stars, which help them to hunt, farm and thrive – and they often live life far more peaceably than human societies that are supposed to be more 'civilized'.

Nowadays the work of the kabbalist is said to be to bring spirituality into the city and into the complex everyday life of modern humanity. Using kabbalistic principles helps people to find their own faith by showing that a generic 'God' can be honoured outside traditional sacraments. It can also demonstrate to us that God is omnipresent: all that exists is divine and we all have that core of divinity within us, no matter how we behave externally. We are not required to love each other's outer manifestations, but to honour the inner core of a person, which is linked to our own. Just doing that helps to transform our perception in any case.

The universal law of cause and effect is not just something that is talked about in theory. It applies to every particle of life – whether that is a molecule in a rock or a giant corporation. As people progress along a spiritual path they begin to observe this law in all things.

As beings coexisting with God, human beings are co-creators. Whatever we think or do has an effect, no matter how small. The equation that brings thought into actual manifestation is said to be Thought + Belief + Feeling + Action = Result. Without all these components, we will not create a final outcome – which is a fortunate thing. However, by combining these components (which involves drawing down energy from all four worlds, see page 19), we really can create situations or events in the physical world.

Yesod does much of our creating by default. If we give our attention to the griefs and cares of others and believe that the same will happen to us, then we are in danger of drawing similar experiences. The same thing occurs if we have a belief system that life is good, prosperous and happy. However, today's society does not help us foster such a belief, so it usually requires conscious use of Tiferet to create the good things in life consistently.

The work of UNIFICATION

Traditions such as Kabbalah can be very powerful because they demonstrate how all angles of belief can be integrated to make religion inclusive.

The Latin word *religio* means 'I bind'. It is apparently intended to mean 'I bind back to myself', but all too often people become bound into one specific mould, to the exclusion of all others. There are approximately six billion people in the world, all of whom are unique. A kabbalist might say that once we realize our individuality instead of following the herd, then there will need to be six billion different religions. No one of us can be expected to see the world from the same viewpoint as anyone else – unless, that is, we are not thinking for ourselves. Every one of us is conscious only of what we call reality from our own viewpoint (whether that is opinion-by-default or true knowledge).

If you place a vase of mixed flowers on a table and ask four people on different sides of the table to describe what they see, they will all come up with a different combination of flowers. Two may see roses, where a third sees only carnations and ferns, and a fourth sees roses and carnations. To a developed kabbalist, fighting wars over religion is similar to getting into a fight about whether there is one rose, two roses or no roses at all in that vase.

True mystics – whether they are kabbalists, Sufis, Christians, Hindus, Shintos, Sikhs, pagans or 'New Agers' – can all feel comfortable together because they are working from the *inner* tradition rather than the outer. Even if their traditions do not agree in every detail, the structure is similar enough for fascinating discussion, rather than opposition.

A vase of flowers looked at from two different sides can look completely different. It is the same with our perception of truth.

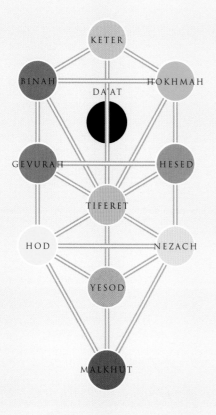

Exercise
Walking The Tree

Find a place where you have enough space to lay out the sefirot of the Tree of Life on the floor. Cut out paper circles, or use stones or plates, to represent each sefirah. For Da'at, use something that is different from all the other sefirot.

○ **Look at the Tree of Life you have created. Are the symbols you have chosen for the sefirot all the same size and colour?** Your first response to that may be that you do not have ten stones or plates of the same colour or size; even so, the point where you have placed each one will be significant to your own personal Tree.

○ **Are any of the symbols that you have used particularly prominent and, if so, to which sefirah does this relate?** This will tell you which area of your life is using up most energy. Also notice which paper circles, stones or plates you find attractive and which unattractive. This will reveal which inner energies you enjoy using and which you do not.

○ **Now stand at the place of Malkhut and close your eyes. Say the name of that sefirah to yourself ten times and see what thoughts arise.** Repeat this with all the sefirot, walking from Malkhut to Yesod, then to Hod, Nezach, Tiferet, Gevurah, Hesed, Da'at, Binah, Hokhmah and Keter. (When you get to Da'at, turn round and face Malkhut to experience the different essence of this sefirah; then, when you move on to Binah, turn to face the top of the Tree again.)

○ **Assess whether you felt most comfortable on either of the side pillars or in any of the sefirot.** Which was your favourite place to stand in? If there was one sefirah that felt particularly uncomfortable, that represents the part of your life that is most out of balance and in need of healing.

A simple way to start the healing process is to return to the sefirah in question and stand there, stilling your mind and thinking the words 'Peace, harmony, laughter, love' for about five minutes.

Exercise
Meditating on the Tree

Sit comfortably and relax as much as you can. Close your eyes and imagine the Tree of Life in front of you. Each of the sefirot is a circular door.

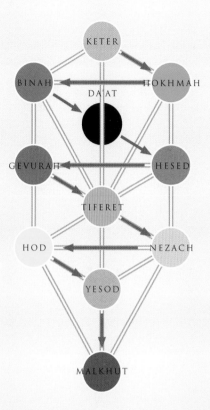

- ○ **Open each door in turn, from Malkhut to Keter, reversing the Lightning Flash (see right), and note whether you get an impression of the contents within each sefirah.** If you are a naturally visual person, you may see an image; if you are a kinaesthetic (feeling) person, you may get a sensation; and if you are a clairaudient (hearing) person, you may hear a sound. Do not worry if you see images that are unpleasant; this is just your psyche alerting you to the fact that something needs a little healing.
- ○ **Once you are at Keter, repeat the process by coming back down, but this time use your imagination to clean out each sefirah.** Use whatever seems appropriate and, when you have finished, tell the sefirah that you bless it and that it is becoming healed. Then close the door and move on. Again, don't worry if you cannot do this 'inner cleansing' completely. None of us is perfect and it takes a while to transform ourselves.

If you find that all your sefirot are perfect and need no help at all, it may be that you need to look a little deeper – to see what lies behind the inner door beyond the outer one.

Exercise
Affirmation

Draw one Tree of Life freehand, and then affirm 'I approve of myself' for a period of 24 hours. Then draw a second Tree. You will probably find that you have drawn a very different freehand tree afterwards. The affirmation changes nothing outside of you – but once you change inside, cosmic law responds.

The LEVELS
within us

As a set of universal principles, Kabbalah is both constant and variable. The structure remains the same down the ages, but a more colloquial form can be given to it to make it as fresh and vibrant today as it was 4,000 years ago.

All true spiritual growth requires individuality – the ability to think and make decisions for yourself based on knowledge.

However, putting on the appropriate 'spin' does not change the way the universe works. Kabbalah teaches that it follows a specific mathematical formula based on the levels found in Jacob's Ladder.

Human beings operate on four basic levels, in just the same way that the universe does (see far right). While we are amazing beings of incredible potential, capable of accessing all four worlds (see page 19), we are also a mixture of mineral, vegetable and animal levels, as well as human – and the three other levels have a tendency to resist the development of the human principle.

Three of the levels are a part of nature, and two of them are experienced by all life-forms: the 'animal level' (as its name implies) is experienced by animals as well as humans. None of the levels is judged to be right or wrong within Kabbalah; they are all a part of the creative process.

As human beings on a spiritual path, we have a tough call, because to reach the human level of development we have to step out of nature and go against many of our natural instincts. Even so, most of us are a combination of all four levels, and the task is to balance each one and to ensure that they all serve our spiritual growth.

NATURE

On the kabbalistic Tree of Life, nature is placed in the Assiyatic or physical world (see page 20). As such, it extends into Yezirah (the psychological world) as far as Tiferet. So when we are in our ego-mind around Yesod and anywhere else below Tiferet, we are said to be subject to the forces of nature.

Nature on Earth has a very definite plan. It gives birth, grows, reproduces, nurtures and dies; it buds, blooms, fruits and dies back and then repeats the pattern for as long as it can. When it dies, it decays and returns to the soil to nourish it, so that other natural things can take its place.

Nature requires us to eat, drink, have sex, search for heat and light to experience comfort, and fight when our dwelling place, our source of food, our belief system or our survival are threatened. Nature does not relate to individuals who step out of line and do not do the 'normal' thing – and it has been known to fight back. Natural inclinations, desires and habits that we find pleasant, but know are not doing us any good, can be hard to resist. If our Malkhut demands a bar of chocolate and our Yesod agrees with it, there is going to be quite a fight if Tiferet thinks that chocolate might not be a good idea right now.

Much of humanity tends to be ruled by Yesodic thinking, and our families, friends and colleagues may find our different ideas and beliefs threatening. Many a person embarking on spiritual work has been put off by peer pressure. In the same way, those seeking spirituality may find it easier to get involved with a cult of some kind or a group with a fundamentalist belief system. This means that they can align their Yesod with a strong group-ego so that they feel safe. It also means they do not have to think for themselves.

Kabbalah teaches that all true spiritual growth requires individuality – the ability to think and make decisions for yourself based on knowledge.

Are you a MINERAL person?

Mineral people are basic, simple souls, uninterested in much other than food – and possibly television. They are not interested in relationships, don't socialize with friends or care who is top of the league tables or in the charts and, if they have a job, it is usually one that simply requires them to go through the motions. As such, they are neither happy nor unhappy.

A true mineral person is rare, but most of us have an element of the mineral in us. When we are being particularly stubborn, for example, we are holding fast to one opinion without accepting that there might be any other point of

THE FOUR LEVELS

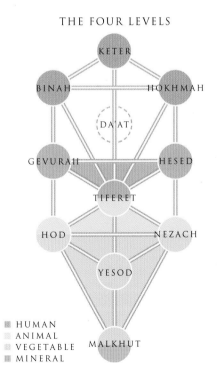

■ HUMAN
  ANIMAL
  VEGETABLE
■ MINERAL

'Vegging out' may be a great way to relax – but if it becomes a habit it will never take you where you want to go in life.

view. Conversely, when we have no opinion about anything, we are also being rather mineral, in not caring to make an assessment or judgement either way.

Mineral reality is defined by Malkhut (the Kingdom, see page 15) – but without the all-important links to any of the other sefirot, especially to Keter. A mineral belief would say that there is absolutely nothing other than that which is before your face; not even scientific proof shown on television could possibly be valid, if it has not been experienced personally.

Are you a VEGETABLE person?

Most of us spend the majority of our lives at the vegetable level. When we get that wonderful new job or step out of line and start spiritual work – rising to the animal and human levels – it is usually our fellow humans at the vegetable level who object most or who point out that we are getting beyond ourselves. Vegetable people do not like being challenged or changed, unless they can see positive and immediate benefits for all.

We all familiar with the concept of 'vegetating': doing nothing much and getting our entertainment passively. To the kabbalist, vegetating is about living in the realms of the sefirot and triads around Yezirah; living life half-asleep in the familiarity of the everyday world. There is nothing wrong with this; it is very comfortable most of the time, even if it does lean towards 'the devil you know'.

At the vegetable level everything feels safe and familiar. We can have a good chat to a friend or a gossip over a drink, if we're feeling down, and go home feeling a lot better. However, if we have just gone over old ground, then we will not have changed anything and the same problem is likely to creep back up on us later. If something recurs that gives us genuine pain, or we have a yearning to move on, it is a sign that we need to give ourselves some kind of kick-start up to another level, even if only for a short time.

Vegetable people want a safe place in which to live; enough to eat and drink; sex and children; and they will push other people out of the way if necessary. Add in football or baseball, soap operas, the daily newspaper and a fortnight in the sun once a year and that is most of us sorted.

To the kabbalist, the vegetable level is very important. We need to grow up strong, be nurtured and taught the ways of the world, and become physically mature as easily as we can. All of that can be – and is – an enjoyable experience, and the challenges it presents are quite enough for most of us. It is only when we can handle life successfully at this level that we are ready to move on and consider a spiritual discipline.

Kabbalah teaches that there are two main dangers to be aware of within the vegetable level:

○ First, the tendency to live life through other people – the great law of cause and effect works even if we are unaware of it, and what we place emphasis on will create life for us, by default. So if life is arranged around television and the local bar, we are likely to be creating in our lives whatever we see and hear around us on the screen or at the bar.

○ Second, vegetable people tend to follow the tribe without thinking for themselves. They are the ones who let dictatorships happen, either because they never saw it coming or because it was much easier for them to be told what to do than to have to think for themselves.

Even if you are on a spiritual path, it is important not to neglect the vegetable level. People who go on prolonged fasts or deny themselves the everyday pleasures of life can become quite out of balance. Kabbalah teaches that working with each of the levels is important, and there are times when a holiday spent 'vegetating' with a few good books by a swimming pool is just as valuable to spiritual growth as following a workshop or studying a doctrine. The aim of life is happiness, and denying the vegetable level makes that hard.

Are you an ANIMAL person?

Animal people are the hunters and wannabes among us. Politicians, company bosses and the famous are all animal people. We are all prone to a little animal fighting when we need to beat someone else to a particular goal, but most of us don't throw our hearts and souls into the fray all the time.

Where vegetable people exist in the three triads around Yesod, animal people exist in the triad between Hod, Tiferet and Nezach. They are either striving towards physical perfection (the Keter of Assiyah) or psychological balance (the Tiferet of Yezirah). They are the ones who make (and break) the rules.

We all get kicked into the animal triad when there is a crisis – for example, a train crash – and we suddenly experience a situation where Yesod has no frame of reference to follow. At such a time the impulse comes mostly from the Assiyatic, physical aspect of the animal level: 'Get out of the train *now*!'

However, the levels between Yezirah and Assiyah often merge, so that the Crown of the physical world and the Tiferet of the psychological world work together as one. This can lead to the impulse to try and help other people out first – that is how heroes and heroines are born. The animal part of us has great courage, but it can also be foolhardy, depending on the rest of our make-up.

The social and work aspects of our lives reflect the 'animal world' where it is easy to get stressed as we jostle for position and approval.

The human level is purely a state of consciousness rather than a state of nature. Humans can all easily be vegetable, animal and human in swift succession.

The HOD/TIFERET/NEZACH triad is also called the 'Awakening Triad' because that is exactly what we do when we hit a crisis: we 'wake up', even if only briefly. As we touch Tiferet, we are open to help from the higher worlds, via Da'at. We may receive extra courage or strength, and miracles can occur – such as being able to lift a car when a child is trapped underneath – which in normal circumstances would appear to be impossible.

It is the true animal people among us who tend to start wars and run battalions; they are the ones who will stand for Prime Minister or President. They will say they care for the greater good of the people – and they may well do so – but, for the majority of animal people, power is the most important thing. Once an animal person is on top of the heap, he or she will put a lot of energy into remaining there.

Fundamentalists of any kind (whether religious or scientific) are usually animal people and (like politicians) they need plenty of vegetable people to follow them. They provide the ideas and charisma, and the vegetable world's natural inclination to follow like sheep does the rest.

We access our animal level when we need it, although some of us find that easier than others. A parent will often become 'an animal' in order to protect a child. The basic animal instinct, however, is to find a good social place in the herd.

Kabbalah teaches that it is an important step in self-development to find our own place within society and to develop our talents at work and at home. Sometimes this is referred to as 'killing your own lion' – meaning that everyone needs to go out and prove himself or herself in the field, facing up to and over-coming strong opposition.

How to be 'HUMAN'

The human level is represented by the triad of Gevurah, Tiferet and Hesed. It stands outside the physical world of Assiyah, so it is purely a state of consciousness rather than a state of nature. Humans can all easily be vegetable, animal and human in swift succession.

The human level is where we can see our higher purpose – the larger plan of our life – and where we can act unconditionally and dispassionately. The triad of GEVURAH/TIFERET/HESED is known as the 'Soul Triad' and it is this part of humanity that differentiates humans from all other species. At this level, we are co-creators with God. This gives humans the choice of doing pure good or pure evil, so at times it is a heavy burden to bear.

There is an old kabbalistic saying that most people know: 'There is nothing new under the sun.' Generally this is taken to mean that nothing new exists but, kabbalistically, it means that the only new things come from the levels above Tiferet – which represents the Sun in the astrological chart.

It is at the soul level that we can forgive hurts that have been imposed upon us and can look at circumstances differently from the way old habits and patterns have taught us. Those amazing people who genuinely do forgive great wrongs, who work for reparation and redemption and in order to help others who have experienced similar pain, are usually working from the Soul Triad.

Those at the human level can get to be world leaders: Gandhi and Nelson Mandela were both once animal people who transformed themselves into men who genuinely put the good of all before the good of one. Both understood the power of forgiveness. Even so, both must have had their moments of temptation, for power is very seductive.

The secret to being truly 'human', according to Kabbalah, is to be able to balance truth, discernment and loving kindness. We are all capable of being human but, unless we can balance the Soul Triad correctly, we are generally imperfectly human. This carries the danger of swinging from good to evil without realizing it.

One of the kabbalistic secrets to attaining this level is to practise detachment. The idea is that, at the human level, we can see things as they really are – as if we are an eagle flying over the Earth and looking at the whole picture. When we do this we can observe how friends, family or the wider world follow particular patterns, and can make considered judgements on whether we can help them or whether our influence will simply make a situation worse. We can also allow people and situations that we do not like to sort themselves out without our interference.

However, detachment can easily over-balance into being uncaring, and even this far into human development, people on a spiritual path can over-balance. When someone at the human level speaks, people usually listen and are influenced because they can feel the mantle of greatness. But great evil can occur when a person at the human level becomes unbalanced and misuses power, for they may influence the karma of nations. Over the centuries millions have died because a powerful person at the human level (such as Adolf Hilter) slipped over into the dark side.

Over-loving without discipline can also have a catastrophic effect in disempowering people. This imbalance can extend to the point of believing that you should act to save people's souls, even if it means harming their bodies.

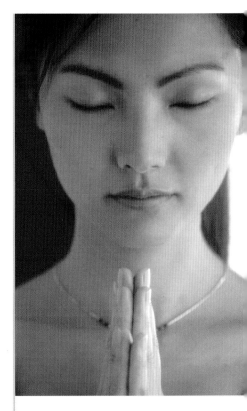

To be human is to be able to go within and look at the world from a detached view where we can see a wider picture away from our personal issues.

However, it is rare that a human being gets to the human level and then over-balances because, as we work our way up the sefirot, the next stage after reaching Tiferet is Gevurah.

This sefirah (see page 16) means discipline, as well as discernment and judgement, and it is also the place of commitment. Most of us are happy to learn about spirituality and to try and live our lives according to its principles, but making a total commitment to it is another matter. Figuratively speaking, to pass Gevurah and enter the Soul Triad for the purpose of living your life at that level is the equivalent of taking holy orders or entering a monastery.

In Kabbalah, the Soul Triad is also referred to as the 'House of Israel' and the levels below it as the 'Children of Israel'. We are nearly all Children of Israel, and Kabbalah teaches that this is how it should be. It is in the everyday play of the animal and vegetable levels that we learn many of the valuable skills we will need when we do, eventually, become enlightened.

The S I D E T R I A D S

A word of explanation may be needed here about the side triads, which carry our unconscious conditioning and impulses.

Kabbalah teaches that the TIFERET/HOD/GEVURAH triad is the place where the emotional judgements and values that we make during our lives are stored. These can be bad or good, according to our experiences and what we make of them.

An example might be a scientist who has had a bad experience of religion and who will put pressure on Tiferet to try to ensure that no further experiences are allowed to change that view. Or it could be just the opposite: a person of faith who has had a bad experience of science and will not allow any new thoughts about that to be processed in order to learn something new. This triad is the place of repression and passive emotional complexes – which can end up being either sensibly cautious or deeply fearful.

On the other side, TIFERET/NEZACH/HESED is the triad of active emotional complexes, which initiate experiences such as falling in love with someone new in order to get over a previous affair. This triad gives us the opportunity to transform emotional patterns and be open to fresh ideas and discoveries, but it can also be overly emotional and excitable and blind to reality.

The other side triads represent our intellectual complexes. The left-hand triad of BINAH/GEVURAH/TIFERET is the place of embedded

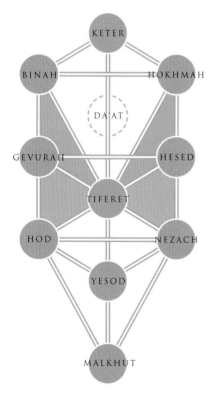

THE SIDE TRIADS

consciousness of our nationality or religion. Even people whose faith has lapsed still keep to many traditions from the religion of their birth because it 'just seems right'.

The right-hand triad of HOKHMAH/HESED/TIFERET focuses on philosophy and ideals; this is where we can throw over all the old ideas for the sake of revolution. Someone with a strong BINAH/GEVURAH/TIFERET triad might be willing to die for their country and beliefs; someone with a strong HOKHMAH/HESED/TIFERET triad might be willing to die as a revolutionary to change the world. But for most of us these triads are simply the source of subconscious inklings of what we think is 'right' and 'wrong'.

Tiferet is in contact with all these triads, but also has access to the higher worlds and to the Soul Triad of free will. It usually struggles to match up all the information and work out what is useful and what is out of date. Given the fact that it is also generally being influenced by Yesod, it is no wonder that life can get confusing. No kabbalist would ever say that being a human being was a soft option.

DIVINITY: what it is and how you can touch it

The highest level that an incarnated human being can reach, according to Kabbalah, is the spiritual triad of BINAH/HOKHMAH/TIFERET. This is the place of revelation and direct experience of God – a place that we may reach for a moment or two in meditation, but that is all.

After the sixth century BCE, followers of the kabbalistic tradition became known as 'Merkabah [Chariot] Riders' because of a dream by the prophet Ezekiel of a chariot ascending up through the four worlds to this triad. Followers of the Merkabah tradition used meditation to ascend through the halls of Heaven, and some even claimed to have seen the image of Adam Kadmon.

In later years Rabbi Moses Cordovero, in *Pardes Rimonim* (see page 12), told of four rabbis who tried to ascend to these highest levels: Rabbi ben Azzai gazed at the Divine Presence and died; Rabbi ben Zoma gazed and went mad; Rabbi ben Acher lost his faith; only Rabbi Akiba ben Joseph entered in peace and left in peace.

The story is told in order to demonstrate how ascension into the higher realms can be dangerous – and should only be attempted when the foundation is strong and the soul is ready. Even today mystical 'Chariot Riders' in the

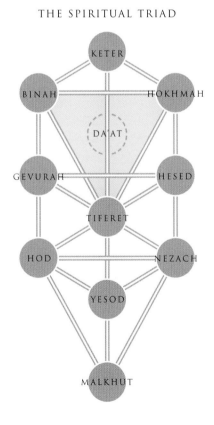

THE SPIRITUAL TRIAD

KETER

BINAH   HOKHMAH

DA'AT

GEVURAH   HESED

TIFERET

HOD   NEZACH

YESOD

MALKHUT

Humanity's issues with divinity may well arise from the fact that we are only looking at two or three of the ten aspects of God.

kabbalistic tradition work in groups, where one soul is thoroughly prepared for ascension while the others keep watch and provide a channel enabling him or her to return to Earth swiftly and safely.

The nature of GOD

In the Torah it says that mankind is made 'in the image of God'. To the kabbalist, this means that we are each made up in exactly the same way as the ten emanations of God in the divine world of Azilut. The idea that God has ten aspects is a strange one for most people, but it may help to explain why there are so many different faiths and ideas about the reality of God.

Humanity's issues with divinity may well arise from the fact that we are only looking at two or three of the ten aspects of God. To a kabbalist, this would mean that we have an unbalanced picture: God as the old father figure… God the Judgemental… God the Merciful, and so on.

It is doubtful that any kabbalist would say that a human being could understand God – it is like piecing together a huge multi-dimensional jigsaw, one so large that you cannot see all of it from one place. However, we can get an idea of how to start to comprehend divinity if we observe the clues in the kabbalistic Tree of Life and Jacob's Ladder.

In the Bible, God told Moses that Its name was I AM. That was extended into I AM THAT I AM. To a kabbalist, this can mean God the Transcendent (the God beyond us) and God the Immanent (the God within us): God at the Keter of Azilut (I AM) extending down the whole of Jacob's Ladder (THAT) to God at the Malkhut of Assiyah (I AM).

Moses was also given a holy name for the Children of Israel to use – the sacred Tetragrammaton, which is written down as YHVH, but which is never pronounced by devout Jews. The Hebrew letters for the Tetragrammaton, when placed vertically, appear to create an image of the Fiery Man: Adam Kadmon himself.

The Hebrew names of the ten aspects of divinity are:

- ○ EHYEH *I AM*
- ○ YAHVEH To Become
- ○ ELOHIM Many Gods
- ○ EL God the Great
- ○ YAH God the Just
- ○ YAHVEH ELOHIM The Holy One
- ○ ELOHIM ZEVAOT Hosts of Elohim

○ YAHVEH ZEVAOT Hosts of Yahveh
○ EL HAI SHADDAI Almighty Living God
○ ADONAI My Lord.

The Ten Commandments follow the same pattern down the Lightning Flash (see page 15) of the four worlds and so do the orders of archangels and angels (see page 103) and the human psyche.

Kabbalah says that we can only see God in a partial light – which will be misrepresentative and can easily create a graven image. The third commandment is at Binah, and one of its meanings is that any perception of God carries the danger of idolatry. People, ideas or images from below the point of Keter can be icons (windows to the Divine), but if they are confused with the real thing, they become graven images instead.

The ten main sefirot, which are the ten emanations of God, exist in all four worlds. In Beriah they reflect the perfect idea of divinity in us; in Yezirah they are the fluctuating forms of divinity in us; and in Assiyah they are the physical reality of divinity in us.

The supernal (celestial) triad of BINAH/KETER/HOKHMAH (see page 43) is separated from the lower part of each Tree by Da'at, the black hole. The Da'at of one world is the Yesod of another, and that is another reason why kabbalists call Yesod the Foundation. The ego must be working as the basis/support of truth (Tiferet) in order for the journey through Da'at to be safe. So without a strong spiritual foundation in Beriah, it is hard to move up to the higher worlds through the Da'at of Yezirah. In the same way, without a strong and true Yesod foundation in Yezirah, information transmitted through the Da'at of Assiyah (the physical body) cannot get through. Your body may be trying to tell you that it wants some attention, but you need to be able to hear it.

Kabbalah teaches that divinity exists in everything from the Keter of Keters at the top of Jacob's Ladder to the Malkhut of Malkhuts at the very base. So, for a kabbalist, everything we see and do is a reflection of the Divine. That carries a heavy responsibility, but great joy as well.

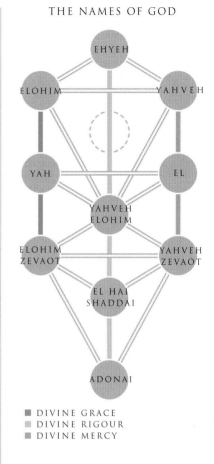

THE NAMES OF GOD

EHYEH

ELOHIM YAHVEH

YAH EL

YAHVEH ELOHIM

ELOHIM ZEVAOT YAHVEH ZEVAOT

EL HAI SHADDAI

ADONAI

■ DIVINE GRACE
▨ DIVINE RIGOUR
■ DIVINE MERCY

WILL

The five triads of the lower part (face) of the Tree of Life are also known as the triads of 'will', equating to levels of our will-power. There are three at the vegetable level, one at the animal level and one at the human level.

A baby may not seem 'will-less' to us but it is only concerned with whether it feels good or bad and it has little idea of how to ask for any specific needs.

Will is seen as very important in Kabbalah, because unless we understand the kind of person we are, it is hard for us to develop the power to access our free will. Free will is the secret to making decisions as an individual, rather than as a conditioned response, and is instrumental in helping us to change our life for the better.

Are you will-less, wilful or willing?

None of us is entirely represented by the characteristics of the triads, for they are archetypes. However, we can see from the characteristics of each level of will, to which one we are most drawn.

WILL-LESSNESS

HOD/YESOD/MALKHUT represents will-lessness. A totally will-less person just drifts though life, taking the path of least resistance and allowing things to happen around himself or herself. Will-less people go where they are told, marry the first convenient person who will have them, have children because they come along or because everyone else does, and may well work at a job they hate because they cannot see any way out of it. Will-lessness is also equated with the first stage of a baby's life, when it has no idea how to ask for what it needs, except by screaming. It does little but wave its arms and legs around, learns to smile when it feels good and sleeps much of the time.

For most of us a tendency towards will-lessness will manifest in a reluctance to get involved in groups, societies or anything that involves time and effort. The motto of someone who tends towards will-lessness could well be 'Anything for a quiet life'.

WILFULNESS

The MALKHUT/YESOD/NEZACH triad represents wilfulness. Wilful people demand what they want from life and go for it, regardless of others. They are different from animal people in that their desires are simply desires; nothing is planned out carefully with a view to overcoming opposition and improving status permanently; it is more a matter of 'I want that *now*'. Wilful people are likely to have more accidents than any other kind because they act before they think, rushing in where angels fear to tread; the word 'tact' does not register in their minds.

In a baby this equates to the stage of the 'terrible twos' when the child is mobile enough to reach for what it wants and may have tantrums when it does not get its own way. Some kabbalists believe that humanity as a whole is at this stage of development.

Most people have moments of wilfulness: we may feel particularly stubborn about something, or adamant that we must have our latest desire at this very moment. We may also be convinced that we are right about something, even if the facts do not back us up.

WILLINGNESS

The HOD/YESOD/NEZACH triad represents willingness. Willing people help everyone else out; they go to workshops and offer to assist, whether by making tea or putting out the chairs. They are also the ones who take the minutes at meetings. They take in every word and say how very transformational the seminar was, but they often find it hard to ground the information in order to make it work for them.

Kabbalistically, the reason is that this triad has no direct link to Malkhut. It is very hard for willing people to make things happen, but they are good at balancing the two side pillars (see page 18); they can see both sides of an

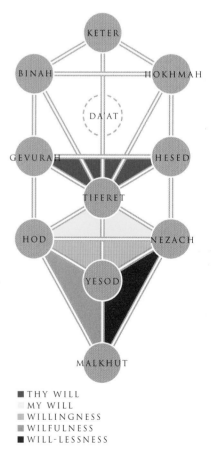

THE LEVELS OF WILL

■ THY WILL
MY WILL
▨ WILLINGNESS
▩ WILFULNESS
■ WILL-LESSNESS

argument and they are excellent at soothing over trouble. Willing people often feel quite scared inside because they sense, subconsciously, that they are in a kind of limbo without any direction of their own.

There is one thing at which willing people excel – being second-in-command. They understand about discipline and, if they can find an animal-person boss who values their intense loyalty, both parties will benefit.

For a child, willingness represents the first learning phase when they have to follow school rules and learn how to behave properly. If parents have not taught children about boundaries, this vital phase of life may not be addressed properly, which can lead to problems later on. People who have never worked out this phase, but who then go on to become animal people, may achieve their 15 minutes of fame – but little more, because they have no grounding in discipline.

My WILL

HOD/TIFERET/NEZACH is the triad of 'my will'. This can go two ways, and transforming it from the first to the second stage is vital for spiritual growth. The first stage is almost akin to wilfulness in that it is purely animal: trying to get to the top of the heap. However, it is successful because this triad does have discipline and perseverance, unlike the Malkhut/Yesod/Nezach triad.

As the top sefirah of this triad is the Keter of Assiyah (see page 20), the person expressing 'my will' does have the ability to ground himself or herself. In fact, they can be physically powerful people with a great presence.

The second stage involves transforming the purely physical, Assiyatic desire for power into a psychological search for the self. For most of us, the 'my will' phrase of growth is the one where we find out who we really are and what we want from life, as opposed to what we were always told we would – or should – want.

This is also the level of will-power: making a decision and sticking to it.

Thy WILL

To the kabbalist, the importance of developing our own will – and the discipline to use it – becomes more obvious when we get to the Soul Triad of GEVURAH/TIFERET/HESED. This represents 'thy will' and it is the point where we understand that God knows better than we do, and can see the wider plan and, if we make intelligent choices, will help us to achieve a life of happiness and spiritual growth. The goal is to use our own will-power to do simultaneously what we judge to be 'right' (Gevurah) and 'merciful' (Hesed).

If we have not developed our own will in the Hod/Tiferet/Nezach triad, then we simply cannot access this level, no matter how many workshops we attend or how many gurus we follow.

Trial by jury demonstrates the importance of these levels of will. The court itself is at Malkhut (physical world) and the defendant at Yesod (his or her foundation is being called into question). The witnesses are at Hod (prosecution) and Nezach (defence). The jury sits at Tiferet, listening to the prosecution counsel (Gevurah) and defence counsel (Hesed); the judge advises from Keter, with the benefit of the written law (Binah) and his or her own insight (Hokhmah).

The jury must have the will-power to focus on the information given to them and to assess it impartially, instead of working on prejudices learnt from childhood and other aspects of the outside world. However, they also have to take the judge's points into account. These views will include knowledge of the law and tradition, about which the jury may know nothing – and which may even go against the grain. However, they must accept this higher will and apply it in making their decision, in order for there to be a fair trial.

In the same way, if we want to do God's will, we need to have the discipline to carry it out. It is all very well receiving guidance in meditation – but we have to follow it through.

A developed kabbalist does not see it as a problem to subject himself or herself to God's will as an act of discipline. He or she understands that the Divine will only give experiences that will assist in spiritual growth. It is also understood that, if those are challenging, perfect help will be available to aid them in resolving the issues peacefully.

For the rest of us there is a kabbalistic motto: 'Keep practising!'

Are you a thinker, a feeler or an actor?

In kabbalistic terms, most of us conform to one of three basic types: thinkers, feelers and actors. The three triads around Yesod also represent these three archetypes, and our astrological Moon sign often shows which type we are. Fire and Earth signs are generally 'actors'; Air signs are usually 'thinkers'; and Water signs are normally 'feelers' (see page 51).

You can have some fun with this , working out questions to establish what type your friends and relations are. For example: Your house is on fire. Do you: call the fire brigade? (Fire – actor); put the fire out? (Earth – actor); panic? (Water – feeler); or wonder how it got started? (Air – thinker).

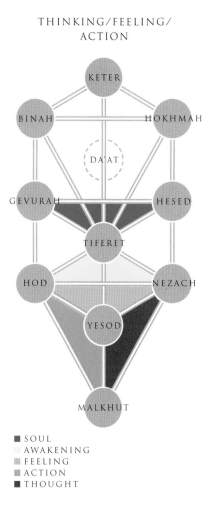

THINKING/FEELING/
ACTION

KETER

BINAH   HOKHMAH

DA'AT

GEVURAH   HESED

TIFERET

HOD   NEZACH

YESOD

MALKHUT

■ SOUL
  AWAKENING
▦ FEELING
■ ACTION
■ THOUGHT

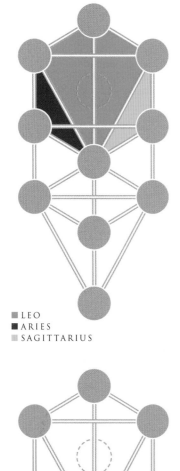

■ LEO
■ ARIES
■ SAGITTARIUS

■ PISCES
□ CANCER
■ SCORPIO

Using ASTROLOGY

The modern kabbalist can draw on centuries of astronomical and astrological knowledge of the workings of the planets in our solar system. The two systems work together in perfect harmony, each helping to clarify the principles of the other. If you already have your own astrological chart, you can plot it on the Tree of Life to give you a head-start in assessing which levels and which sefirot on the Tree will prove to be your strengths and weaknesses (see page 55). If you don't have your own chart, you can obtain a basic computer-generated one for free on the Internet.

The elements are closely linked to the astrological signs:

○ The FIRE signs of the zodiac are: Leo, Sagittarius and Aries.
○ The WATER signs are: Pisces, Cancer and Scorpio.
○ The AIR signs are: Gemini, Libra and Aquarius.
○ The EARTH signs are: Taurus, Virgo and Capricorn.

There are also three different astrological divisions – known as quadruplicities – that have to be added to this equation; they are the Cardinal, Fixed and Mutable aspects of the signs of the zodiac. Cardinal signs are the initiators that herald the changing of the seasons; Fixed signs are the steady, reliable types that hold energy stable; Mutable signs are the ones that are flexible, dissolving energy so that another change can be heralded. This aspect can best be seen in the alternating seasons of the calendar:

○ ARIES (Cardinal) initiates spring.
○ TAURUS (Fixed) maintains it.
○ GEMINI (Mutable) softens the energy to prepare for summer.
○ CANCER (Cardinal) initiates summer.
○ LEO (Fixed) maintains it.
○ VIRGO (Mutable) softens the energy to prepare for autumn.
○ LIBRA (Cardinal) initiates autumn.
○ SCORPIO (Fixed) maintains it.
○ SAGITTARIUS (Mutable) softens the energy to prepare for winter.
○ CAPRICORN (Cardinal) initiates winter.
○ AQUARIUS (Fixed) maintains it.
○ PISCES (Mutable) softens the energy to prepare for spring.

Each quadruplicity needs the other two to create a balanced world. Our natural inclinations towards being animal, vegetable or mineral, wilful, will-less or willing, are all indicated by the placing of the planets in our astrological chart.

People with prominent FIRE in their charts are generally full of bounce and enthusiasm; if fiery elements predominate in the lower face of the Tree (from Malkhut to Tiferet), they will generally be actors and will find it fairly easy to work at the animal level.

People with prominent WATER in their charts are generally emotional, loving and helpful; if watery elements predominate in the lower face of the Tree, they will normally be feelers and, unless they have a good smattering of Earth or Fire to balance them out, will find it challenging to be animal people. However, they will attack if threatened.

People with prominent AIR in their charts are generally full of ideas, but are very changeable and without the will-power to put ideas into action. If airy elements predominate in the lower face of the Tree, they will generally be thinkers but, unless they also have Earth or Fire in their chart, it will be hard for them to be successful animal people as they will not have sufficient commitment to make their ideas become reality.

People with prominent EARTH in their charts are generally strong, reliable, stubborn and not to be moved from their chosen path. If earthy elements predominate in the lower face of the Tree, they will usually be actors – albeit slow and solid ones. They will find it quite easy to be animal people, but their progress will be slow and possibly pedantic, without a good smattering of Air, Fire and Water to lighten them up.

To get a clear picture you need to know the placings of all the planets in your chart, and not just your Sun sign, Moon sign and Ascendant. However, knowing just your Sun and Moon signs will give you a fairly good indication of your basic kabbalistic type. For example:

- ○ SUN: Libra (Cardinal – Air).
- ○ MOON: Scorpio (Fixed – Water).

This indicates to a kabbalist that the person in question is not naturally comfortable at the animal level, because their natural impulse to action is not supported by a strong and decisive will. They tend to make idealistic and impractical decisions, and to act on them without due thought about whether or not they will actually work. However, at a vegetable level, their Moon in strong, fixed Scorpio provides a powerful, maintaining structure to help them try again and again. But unless this person uses conscious thought to change the pattern within the animal level, this repeated effort to lift themselves from the vegetable level may lead to feelings of self-hatred and frustration.

THE ASTROLOGICAL SIGNS

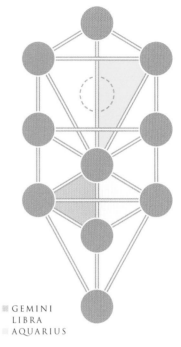

■ GEMINI
  LIBRA
■ AQUARIUS

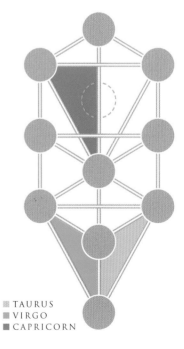

■ TAURUS
■ VIRGO
■ CAPRICORN

THE PLANETS

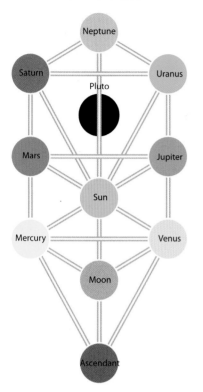

The PLANETS and the levels

In the days before there were powerful telescopes and we knew about the planets of Neptune, Uranus and Pluto, kabbalists allotted only Mercury, Venus, Mars, Jupiter and Saturn, plus the Sun and Moon, to the Yeziratic Tree of Life.

Kabbalists believe that astrology is limited to the Yeziratic world of forms. As such, it has an ongoing effect in Assiyah, but actions from the higher worlds can supersede it at any time. Human free will, also, can overrule astrology. But astrology is a useful tool as a blueprint or plan of life and likely developments.

Until the outer planets were discovered, kabbalists placed the zodiac at Hokhmah, with 'the first swirlings' of the universe at Keter and nothing at all at Da'at – representing the void or the abyss. Nowadays Neptune (planet of the mystical ideal) is placed at Keter; Uranus (planet of revelation and inspiration) rules Hokhmah; and Pluto (the small dark planet, with its strange path that takes it both inside and outside the orbit of Neptune) is placed at Da'at (see left). These three planets are known as 'the trans-personal planets' and, although their placing is important in an astrological chart, they are not particularly helpful in understanding the levels within us and how we respond in everyday life. The other planets are placed as follows:

MALKHUT: The Earth

This is also known as the Ascendant. It represents the mineral level of life, our physical reality, our survival instincts and our physical appearance. Accurate knowledge about this part of us is difficult to access unless we know our time of birth. However, the Ascendant will have a large say in what we look like physically, and whether we appear to be an animal person (with a vibrant, imposing face), a vegetable person (with a softer, more malleable face) or a mineral person (with a set, steady and perhaps expressionless face).

YESOD: The Moon

This represents the ego or persona at the vegetable level. The Moon fluctuates from visible to invisible, with regular phases that affect life on Earth considerably, from the movement of the tides to the biodynamic system of planting and harvesting crops. Because the Moon is so mutable, it is important for us to understand its movements so that they can be utilized to serve us. For the kabbalist, lack of knowledge of the Moon – and therefore of the ego – will undercut our best efforts to live a happy life because we neither know nor understand the foundation that is supporting us. Where our Moon is placed in our astrological chart will indicate whether our Yesod is easy or hard to use as the support on which we need to build our self. All the astrological signs have positive and negative aspects and, to the kabbalist, knowledge is the key to using them well.

HOD: Mercury

This is the communicator, the trickster and the source of everyday information. Kabbalistically it is placed at the vegetable level, because Hodian information is heard or read and recycled without knowledge or experience. It can range from old wives' tales to scientific information or the latest batch of jokes. Mercury in a Cardinal Air or Fire sign can indicate a sharp talker and wit, whereas Mercury in a Fixed Earth sign can make for slow comprehension and difficulty in communicating.

NEZACH: Venus

This represents action, sexual impulses, lust and everyday pleasure. Sexuality and desire are at the vegetable level because they are automatic impulses, as opposed to true love and compassion, which come from the human level of the Soul Triad (see page 40).

TIFERET: The Sun

This represents the self at the animal level, with the possibility of rising to the human level. Our goal in life, according to Kabbalah, is to represent the positive aspects of our Sun sign because that is our true self. Understanding the attributes of our Sun sign, and making conscious efforts to act and be like them, is an important first step in becoming who we were meant to be. The negative aspect of Tiferet is pride. Above Tiferet, we are working at the human level and can see how the sefirot here complement the ones below them and expand on their attributes:

GEVURAH: Mars

Although Mars (or Ares) was a fierce fighting god, the principle of this sefirah is essentially passive and is perhaps better represented by the goddess Athene. In Robert Graves's retelling of the Greek myths he says, 'In battle she never loses, even against Ares himself, being better grounded in tactics and strategy, and wise captains always approach her for advice', so Athene is the epitome of the Martial principle. Here at the human level, the Martial principle

The phases of the Moon and its dark side, which is always hidden from our view, demonstrate the nature of the human ego consciousness.

needs to be perfectly balanced by Hesed to work at its best. Gevurah takes information from Hod and considers it, balancing it with understanding from Binah and adding its own discernment.

HESED: Jupiter

This is the jovial king of the gods; its principle is that of loving kindness, and this is the place where the passion and excitement of Nezach can be developed into lasting emotion. It is at the human level – and needs Gevuric Mars to balance it, or it may over-balance into excess.

BINAH: Saturn

This is the place of structure, boundaries and time. Saturn grinds down the inspiration received from Hokhmah, discarding everything that simply will not work. It also provides strength and structure, building strong foundations.

KETER: Neptune

Neptune is traditionally the god of the sea and Keter is the place where we are at the crown of the watery, Yetziratic world of the psyche. There, we can rule it making discerning and compassionate decisions about life, instead of allowing our habits and emotions to rule us. Keter is what is known as the Higher Self, our true being.

Putting our personal chart onto the Tree of Life enables us to see which parts of us feel comfortable or uncomfortable, and how the levels of our psyches work.

For instance, astrologically the sign of Taurus – which is steady, reliable, sensual and passionate, but prone to charge when deeply provoked – is ruled by Venus. If you have a Taurean Nezach, you are likely to be very comfortable, secure in your sexuality and a faithful lover. However, if Mercury was in the sign of Taurus when you were born, then you may have difficulties in communicating. Hod (ruled by Mercury) is all about quicksilver speech and Taurus is not quick off the mark. You may find that you are often tongue-tied or cannot take in a lot of ideas at once.

On the other hand, if Mercury (Hod) was in the sign of Gemini when you were born, you would indeed have a quicksilver tongue! Gemini and Hod love each other. But Venus/Nezach in Gemini is very uncomfortable and you would probably find that you either have many lovers or are much happier talking about sex than doing it.

Putting your chart on the TREE

In the tree opposite you can see the astrological Tree of a woman born with Sun in Taurus, Moon in Scorpio, Mars in Aquarius and Jupiter in Leo.

Kabbalistically, her Sun (Tiferet) opposes her Moon (Yesod) and her Mars (Gevurah) and Leo (Hesed) form a square to both Sun and Moon. All these are challenging astrological aspects.

In a nutshell, the woman's Soul Triad and her Ego are all shouting at each other. The Sun (steady, honest, anything-for-a-quiet-life Taurus) and Moon (paranoid, secretive, devious Scorpio) are both fascinated and repelled by each other and pulling in completely different directions so it will be hard for her to know who's in charge and easy for her to hate herself, especially when she is young. And her Gevurah, Tiferet and Hesed all challenge each other constantly, with Leonine Hesed (the majestic King of Loving Kindness) and Aquarian Gevurah (we'll do it this way because it's different and I say so – except now we won't because I can't be bothered) also contradicting each other all the way and fighting her Yesodic everyday mind.

You could say that it is a very difficult chart but the lovely thing about Kabbalah is that you can see that a chart like this must belong to quite an old soul and both her past life experiences and her current life childhood of learning to live with her own instabilities should have trained her to be able to deal with almost any external situation by being able to see challenges coming. She's perfectly used to being uncomfortable so she could be a great person to have beside you when the chips are down and she will not be afraid to go to hell and back if a single life can be saved.

In her youth, hidden affairs will have been likely (Scorpio Yesod likes both secrets and sex and Gemini Nezach likes to keep things interesting without making commitments) and, with the jiggery-pokery of all the squares, it's likely that she will also have had a changeable career. Her life task is to clamber out of that mess to become a steady, reliable Taurean with a strong, jovial and sometimes quirky soul.

However, she could also easily cave in under all the pressure and become a timid and resentful mouse – or self-destruct. The choice, of using her Free Will or not, is up to her. This particular woman chose a life-partner with an entire Soul-Triad in Taurus. He is able to hold her steady and stabilise her while she can intrigue and stimulate him.

A CHART ON THE TREE

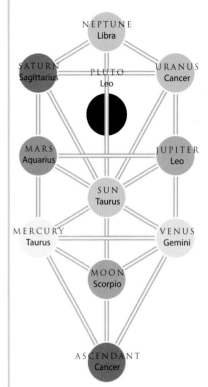

Studying a spiritual book or learning a subject you are genuinely interested in is a form of contemplative meditation.

MEDITATION made easy

The purpose of meditation is to clear the mind of the everyday clutter and chatter that circulates inside our heads. Most of this comes from the levels around Yesod, and may manifest in the form of voices talking to us, self-criticism, songs-on-the-brain or list-like repetition. These voices prevent us from hearing the 'still small voice within', which can guide us more successfully than everyday chatter at the vegetable level. Clearing our minds through meditation for just a few minutes each day is as beneficial as a good night's sleep.

There are three main types of meditation: active, contemplative and devotional. For the beginner it is a good idea to start with the one that suits your astrological and emotional type. Actors (Earth and Fire signs) will enjoy active meditation; thinkers (Air signs) will focus well on contemplative meditation; and feelers (Water signs) will be most at home with devotional meditation.

However, to create balance it is a good idea to practise all three forms – and, when the techniques are familiar, even to focus on the one that is least preferred. This will help to coordinate the sefirot and the levels within your own personal Tree of Life.

ACTIVE meditation

This is meditation with movement and involves total concentration on what you are doing. Most successful athletes practise active meditation during a race. A dressage rider or showjumper is practising active meditation by becoming one with his or her horse. You can actively meditate while walking, swimming, dancing, horseriding, cycling or even doing the washing up.

The secret is to focus entirely on your actions, to the extent that everything else drops away and you feel lifted to a higher level. The emotional level that is achieved generally feels like being in the eye of a storm: everything else appears to be moving while you are standing still.

It is wise to use movement as active meditation only when you are in a 'safe' space – that is, away from outside influences that could knock you off balance. The experienced meditator, deep within his or her self, can still sense potential outside threats, such as another person coming too close. However, for the beginner it is best to practise with someone else observing you.

CONTEMPLATIVE meditation

This is a way of clearing the mind of thought through thought! Everyday thoughts from Hod and Yesod are superseded by conscious study or listening to a guided meditation. Revising for an exam can be a kind of contemplative meditation – as is becoming totally absorbed in a good book. Again, the secret is to still the mind to all thoughts while concentrating on the task in hand.

With guided meditation you listen to some kind of story that encourages you to go on a journey or have a particular experience in your mind. You clear your mind of everyday thoughts as you become involved in the story that you are living inside yourself.

Kabbalistic guided meditations take us up the Tree or the Ladder, to observe either the workings of the psyche or our place on the path of life. Such focus clears space within the mind for intuition, or even to enable outside help from our guides and angels (see page 100) to reach us.

DEVOTIONAL meditation

Devotional meditation involves prayer, listening to music or specific sounds, or sitting in complete silence. It is the form of meditation that requires the most will-power because there is nothing in particular to hold our attention. Focusing entirely on prayer or music are the easier options; stilling the mind while in total silence is a great challenge for many.

For most people, even experienced meditators, there is a regular battle to be fought with Yesod when we try to be still and silent, because it is a discipline that denies the ego any part. All kinds of thoughts can fly into our heads unbidden and trap us into following them until we are deep in thought, instead of meditating. However, it is worth trying to still the mind even if only for a minute at a time, just to see how it resists.

Painting, singing, playing a musical instrument and doing calligraphy are often thought to represent a combination of active, devotional and contemplative meditation.

FREE WILL

Free will is when we make conscious choices about our life. It is what makes people stand out in the crowd, turn away from the path that everyone else is taking and live an individual life.

Free will is unique to humans. Animals do not have the levels of consciousness to make decisions in the same way that a human does. For example, a dog given two bowls of food to choose from will select first the one it prefers on the basis of scent, taste and experience. A human, on the other hand, can

Devotional meditation takes great discipline in order to clear the mind of all external thought.

For most people there is a regular battle to be fought with Yesod when we try to be still and silent.

either make a similar decision to the dog, for the same reasons, or can consider other aspects as well (such as whether he or she needs the food, approves of the food ethically or nutritionally, and whether somebody else needs it more).

Kabbalah teaches that if we do not rule our own bodies and minds from Tiferet and the Soul Triad, then they will rule us. We have the choice to live life on automatic or to apply discipline in order to direct our life as we wish it to be. But the majority of our thoughts and the decisions we take are made from the vegetable level around Yesod, and are automatic .

You can test out your everyday ability to access your free will by disciplining yourself to meditate. If you cannot even remember that you were intending to meditate, or your instinctive reaction is 'But I don't *want* to meditate', then your free will is probably being overruled by your Yesod.

It is easy to confuse this with rebellion or a sense of revolution. However, most people who focus their life on reform, environmental issues or living differently may start out by accessing their free will, but end up in a group or society that lives life in the same way as they do; they therefore return to automatic – albeit an unusual form of automatic. A useful key here is to observe whether the 'alternative' lifestyle is being lived with grace and enjoyment or is fuelled by anger and resentment against the actions of others.

It is virtually impossible to access our free will all the time. For a start, we need our Yesod to guide us through the day, and it is much easier to rely on old thought patterns and habits to make decisions than to start from scratch.

Kabbalah also teaches that our range of free will is limited according to our destiny, astrology and situation. It is just possible that a prisoner sentenced to solitary confinement for life in Afghanistan may, one day, appear in high society in London as a famous concert pianist, but it is highly unlikely. He or she can, however, use his or her free will in deciding how best to live life in jail and what benefit may be created for everybody concerned in a difficult situation.

It takes a conscious act of free will to decide to be happy in difficult circumstances against the odds. But it can be done. This is why free will is accessible only from the level of the Soul Triad. It takes the ability to view the wider picture to be able to apply such discipline.

To practise accessing free will, the kabbalist has to learn not to react to everyday news and to think laterally. To choose positive thought in a negative time may be a good example of using free will – however, it could also be a learnt reaction from Yesod in order to hide emotions and fears. Every person has a different make-up and a different way of being individual.

Quite often our first experience of free will may appear to be negative – we do not want to do something, and we do not see why we *should* do that something, but an inner voice prompts us to alter our mind-set and be brave enough to try. Signs to look out for when attempting to access our free will are:

○ The willingness to align ourselves with God's will rather than our own, even if it goes against the grain.

○ The desire and knowledge to ensure that any decision is both fair and kind.

○ The will-power to take a decision that may make us unpopular.

○ The willingness to wait until we have all the facts available instead of rushing to make a decision.

○ A deep inner prompting as to when the time is right or wrong to act or speak.

○ The ability to admit that we have been wrong and to radically rethink our position.

○ The willingness to let other people act in whatever way they please, without being affected by it ourselves.

○ The ability to see through appearances to the heart of the matter.

○ The willingness to let go of people, situations and feelings that no longer enhance our life.

Acquiring free will is a life's work. Kabbalah teaches that we are not expected to operate from such a high level all the time – we would be exhausted. But just knowing that we can lift ourselves up in times of peace or crisis is one of the greatest blessings there is.

Kabbalah teaches that our range of free will is limited according to our destiny, astrology and situation in life.

Being TRUE
to yourself

The first thing to do in being true to yourself is to acknowledge that there is a battle between the ego and the self. Just because we have always done something in a certain way does not mean that it is necessarily right.

Kabbalah is very different from eastern traditions such as Buddhism, which tend to believe that the ego should be suppressed or destroyed. To the kabbalist, the ego is a vital component in self-development. It needs to be trained – and all too often it is in charge when it should be second-in-command – but without it we would find it impossible to live our lives comfortably.

When Yesod (the Foundation, or place of the human ego) is in balance, it is the best servant that Tiferet (Beauty, or the place of the true self) could ever ask for; it supports and advises us from its great wealth of background information, but it accepts whatever our self decides and stands right behind the self, whatever the outcome. In fact Yesod is more than a servant; it is a friend – and a very good friend at that. It is just a slightly younger friend who has to be nurtured and guided, instead of one who bosses us around.

Yesod does everything on automatic. It is generally fully formed by the time we are seven years old, so we learn how to react from a very early age – and we are still using that same information to rule our lives 20 or 30 years later. The Jesuits are famous for the phrase 'Give me a boy until he is seven and I have him for life', and there is a great deal of truth in it.

Yesod can be retrained; all you need to know right now is that it already is trained, but probably not in a way that is helpful to your spiritual growth. When you start to reprogramme it, Yesod will most likely resist and tell you that you are wrong to want to change things at all!

However, the ego can be much more cunning than that. It may appear to agree with you perfectly, then engineer things so that you are always too busy to do the work to retrain it. Yesod is also very good at persuading you that you cannot attend a particular workshop, because of family commitments or because you are too tired. Yesod is the part of you that reacts negatively to something new in an old routine, or to a new teaching that overturns something you learnt before.

Yesod is also the part of you that chooses what to wear in the morning and the way you appear to the world. It is your persona or mask, and it can either show you off to best advantage or ruin your chances – according to the orders it received from your parents, teachers, peers and yourself when you were a child. If it was safe to shine then, Yesod will make you shine now; if not, it will hide you whenever it can, whether it does this through the clothing you wear, your expression or your actions.

When you learn to drive a car or ride a horse, it is all new and sometimes frightening. You have to be wide awake and observant – and Yesod cannot handle that; it is not its job to do so. Anything innovative has to be handled by Tiferet. However, once you have learnt the skill, you hand the operation over to Yesod, to be repeated on automatic until further notice. You can often drive quite a long way and have no idea whatsoever how you got where you did – because your mind was miles away, and Yesod was driving without consulting you, because it can do it so well. Unfortunately, if you let it, Yesod will also run your entire life, choose your partner, work, holidays and lifestyle – unless you stand up for yourself and use your free will to change things.

Whenever there is a crisis, Yesod retreats and Tiferet is back in charge. That is one of the reasons why the spirit of endurance that prevails in wartime is so powerful – people are shocked into their real selves and achieve miracles, through a partnership of strangers, that they would never have considered possible without such a challenging situation.

In Kabbalah, crisis is often called the 'wake-up call'. Many crises might be avoided if we kept ourselves slightly awake. Marital breakdown, accidents, sickness, job loss and other calamities are usually horrifying only if we did not see them coming. If we saw them coming and did nothing, that was probably a Yesodic decision – and not a helpful one.

Our habits and beliefs were usually formed many years ago and may not serve to bring us feelings of safety and happiness any more.

When we get jolted out of Yesod and are left standing alone and frightened in a completely new situation, we have to wake up and choose new responses. Just how long we stay awake is up to us. Many a good intention has been formed at the funeral of someone who dies young and whose death has brought our own mortality home to us: 'I will spend more time with the family'; 'I will take that holiday/sabbatical'; 'I will take the plunge and get married'; 'I will look for a new job.'

Six weeks later most people are safely half-asleep again at the vegetable level. They may have voiced their intentions to loved ones or colleagues and had them squashed; they may simply have forgotten them. Or Yesod – perhaps working with the subconscious fears in the Gevurah/Tiferet/Hod triad and with the deep conditioning of the Gevurah/Binah/Tiferet triad – may have conspired against the individual: 'Safer to stay with the Devil you know ...'; 'safer not to rock the boat ...'; 'too many other people might get cross ...'

Following the 'PATH OF HONESTY'

Understanding the paths between the sefirot on the kabbalistic Tree of Life would require a separate book, with comprehensive explanations of the meaning of the 22 Hebrew letters and, for the modern kabbalist, study of the tarot. Most developed kabbalists would say that it is best to fully understand the sefirot, the levels and the astrological interpretations before starting to study the paths in detail. However, it can be useful to start working with the paths simply as linking points between the sefirot, showing which aspects of the Tree of Life are in direct communication with the others.

One of the most important of paths is the one between Yesod and Tiferet. It is called the 'Path of Honesty' and it is the all-important key to working the two sefirot together. If you are truly honest with yourself about a situation, both of these sefirot are likely to be in balance. If you cannot see the wood for the trees (or perhaps a kabbalist should say 'cannot see the Trees for the wood'), then Yesod is refusing to let you get to your real self.

For example, if a relationship has broken down in exactly the same way as a previous one did, Yesod is likely to tell you that it is not your fault. However, Tiferet may feel uneasy because it has begun to observe a pattern and wonder what its responsibility was in those relationships. Tiferet is good at responsibility; it has the ability to respond rather than simply react. Through the Path of Honesty, Tiferet and Yesod can work together to decide what the pattern is and why an almost identical relationship to one that had ended badly was

THE PATH OF HONESTY

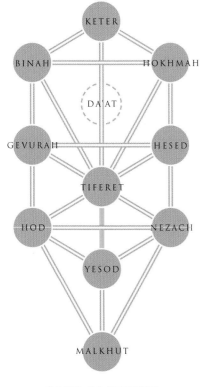

KETER

BINAH   HOKHMAH

DA'AT

GEVURAH   HESED

TIFERET

HOD   NEZACH

YESOD

MALKHUT

■ PATH OF HONESTY

accepted as a good idea. Then, when both sefirot have assessed the situation, a decision can be made to avoid a recurrence.

It is our choice: wake up, or stay asleep and stuck in the same old mould. This path is said to be the place where Lucifer, the fallen angel, lives in order to tempt humanity. And honesty is often much more difficult than it seems. Lucifer is very cunning and will not tempt us with the obvious; instead he will use our pride and vanity (the flip-side of the truth and beauty of Tiferet) to trip us up. It is easy to convince ourselves that we are being totally honest about a situation, but quite often we are subconsciously interpreting it to suit our own ends.

As Kabbalah is an oral tradition, it is often taught in groups and it is helpful to have companions who can see more clearly than we what is going on in our lives and can advise us. It is also useful to refer to our personal astrology and note the negative aspects of both our Sun and Moon signs (see page 52). These will tell us the places where we are most tempted to delude ourselves – and others.

Why DISCIPLINE does not have to be a bogey-word

Most people, even those on a spiritual path, would like life to be easy. It would be lovely if blessings just fell into our lap. One of the great secrets of Kabbalah is that if we take the time and trouble to practise discipline, we make it much more likely that blessings will do just that.

Gevurah (Judgement, or the place of discipline and discernment) is linked directly to Binah (Understanding), Hesed (Loving Kindness), Tiferet and Hod (Reverberation, or the place of communication and information). It is an important balancing place, and a filter that can – and should – make all the really important decisions in our lives, instead of our everyday mind at the vegetable level.

Some of us have a stronger Gevurah than others. A Piscean, watery, Mutable Mars will always have trouble making decisions and disciplining itself, whereas a Capricorn, earthy Mars will not only lay down the law, but will see nothing beyond the law. An Aquarian Mars will tend to be overly idealistic and unpredictable, whereas a Scorpionic Mars will have a sting that makes people jump to attention.

Your Gevurah is the place where your soul level will tell you what your true self believes to be illegal, unkind, unworthy – or just plain wrong. An

Sometimes the truth is hard to hear and difficult to face up to. It is important to be able to assess what is real and what is not.

out-of-balance Gevurah may also tell you that you are just too scared to risk something, when with a little effort you could have done it. However, an in-balance Gevurah will hone and polish an idea or a plan until it shines and you can see exactly how it can and should work.

If you have trouble disciplining yourself or others, it is useful to look along the paths from Gevurah to see which other sefirot can help you. For example, you can draw on the energy of Tiferet to hear what the still, calm voice within you is saying; link that inner voice to Binah to understand just why it might be saying that; then link to Hod in order to explain it. You can also use the path to Hesed, because your Jupiter wants you to look good and will therefore throw in its energy to help. Sometimes all that is needed is a small amount of self-knowledge. Conscious knowledge of our inner strengths and weaknesses represents more than half the battle in solving the issues within us. Knowing that discipline is a problem and calling on the other aspects to help can become a game – and the end results of honing ourselves are well worth the effort involved.

Killing with **KINDNESS**: the importance of balance in our lives

Just as discipline can be a problem with an out-of-balance Gevurah, so over-kindness can be an Hesedic issue that a kabbalist needs to address. When people come into spiritual work it is often because they want to help others and the planet. In fact, the goal of spiritual work for the kabbalist is to perfect the self, not others. This is not as selfish as it sounds; Kabbalah teaches that we cannot help, guide or lead others until we have addressed the issues within us and can lead from a place of knowledge and experience, and not just of good-will and information. In essence, the job is to lead by example, but many of us mistake continual positive thinking and generosity for unconditional love.

Doing too much for others disempowers them so that they do not know how to take care of themselves properly. It can also control them: offering love where it is not needed or wanted can engulf those who do not know how to refuse it. In the New Age this is sometimes seen in the obligatory hugs given at workshops – many people feel that to refuse such a hug would demon-strate that they are not loving and evolved people, whereas the kabbalistic view is that imposing a hug where it is not wanted or needed is the aspect that is out of balance. Often people offer love to others in order to feel good about themselves – and that is not unconditional love.

The secret of true kindness is to do what the other person needs, not what will make us feel good about helping them.

Hesed (Loving Kindness, or the place of unconditional love and mercy) is ruled by Jupiter, the planet that also rules tumours. In Yezirah, this is at the level of the human breasts. It is interesting that, in holistic medicine, cancer is commonly thought of as a disease of 'nice' people: those who don't use the word 'No'.

The heart, too, is at the level of the Soul Triad of Gevurah/Tiferet/Hesed, and much heart disease reputedly stems from either a congested (Gevurah) or over-expanded (Hesed) heart.

Whether we have tendencies towards a particular disease depends on our genetic make-up, our diet and our environment, but holistic medicine and Kabbalah both agree that we can help ourselves psychologically and spiritually to minimize the risks.

Why we fear LOSING CONTROL: and what happens when we do

There is a distinct difference between control and power. Power is a function of the right-hand pillar and control a function of the left-hand pillar. The advertising phrase 'Power is nothing without control' sums it up. The power in an internal combustion engine will have no effect unless it is compressed and filtered (that is, controlled). Similarly, genius at times needs a strong hand to hold it back. A magnificent football team of extroverts needs a Gevuric manager to make them train properly and use their talents to the full.

Some people live life in an uncontrolled manner – and the Yesod of society clamps down on them whenever it can. But for the most part, people tend to overuse rather than underuse control. Kabbalists are taught that there are two forms: control through discipline and control through love. Both forms operate from the Soul Triad and can be highly effective or, if over-applied, destructive.

Control through discipline trains us to use our talents wisely and not to overstep the mark; over-control through discipline stunts our development.

Control through love guides us with gentleness and gives us positive examples to live by. Over-control through love either makes us dependent, because we are never allowed to work or think for ourselves, or manipulates our feelings of love to make us behave in a certain way because others would be hurt if we did not.

We have all heard the phrase 'If you really loved me, you would...' This is the Hesedic, destructive control that calls on guilt. However, the most common kind of control is directing the way our life operates from day to day. This

Control through discipline trains us to use our talents wisely and not to overstep the mark.

To a kabbalist, the word 'should' is a warning light that preconceived notions are being used over free will or considered opinion.

comes from a combination of Yesodic habit patterns and beliefs in how it 'should be', from the triad of Binah/Tiferet/Gevurah, as opposed to straight discipline from Gevurah. It can be summed up by the word 'should' (as in 'I should' or 'you should').

To a kabbalist, the word 'should' is a warning light that preconceived notions are being used over free will or considered opinion. 'Should' is a useful word for beating ourselves up – not to mention beating other people up. Tiferet does not operate on 'should'; a good phrase to use instead might be: 'If I really wanted to I could'. This raises the issue to our consciousness for a considered opinion. Letting go of the 'shoulds' in our life (wherever possible) allows us to expand our consciousness – and view both our own life and that of other people in a different light.

Controlling our life leaves little space to let inspiration through. Letting go of control and allowing ourselves – and others – to be human beings, instead of 'human doings', creates space and shifts us into Tiferet. There we can pause and be open to the blessings that come down to us from Da'at, with the understanding from Binah that solves problems easily and inspiration from Hokhmah to give us a new direction.

Accessing **TRUE POWER**

True power (as opposed to the balance between power and control) comes from being psychologically placed at Tiferet with access to all the other sefirot.

Being placed at Tiferet is like sitting in the centre of a great wheel with the spokes, or paths, leading to all the information and knowledge we could possibly want. Through Da'at, we have access to our higher self and divinity and can draw down the power of the higher worlds. Tiferet is the place of Beauty that links three worlds. Here, an idea or a person becomes 'real', with the opportunity to be physically alive, psychologically balanced and in touch with their spirit. This is the place that we aim to reach in meditation and it is the jumping-off place for contact with the higher worlds. Tiferet is the real you and the only place of true power.

Being **TRUE** to yourself

Nobody can tell you how best to be you. However, study of the sefirot of the Tree of Life will give you important clues in the search for your true self. Here is a summary of kabbalistic guidelines.

○ Each one of us is a cell in the divine body of Adam Kadmon, which means that we all have a destiny and we are all a part of divinity – whatever race, colour or creed we may be.

○ Every human is a composite of genetic structure, inherited memory and experience from past lives – a psychological blueprint defined by the Tree of Life and/or astrology.

○ Every experience in life can be plotted on the Tree of Life so that it can be understood and worked with successfully.

Guide for living:
THE TEN COMMANDMENTS

Our lives become cluttered very quickly and it often seems that there are so many rules and regulations that it is almost impossible to be our true selves in everyday life. We have to make so many decisions that we can lose sight of the basics, but the key to solving virtually every problem is evident in the great law of cause and effect.

Kabbalah uses the Ten Commandments of the Torah/Old Testament as guidelines showing us where this law will most affect us. The commandments represent different levels within us, and applying them can help us to think and live more clearly.

Kabbalah teaches that the commandments were originally intended as guidance for humanity, and not as commands. We are taught that they were given to Moses in two forms: first, the esoteric, engraved in light on sapphire (sefirot); second, 'graven in stone' after Moses threw down and broke the originals because he saw the Israelites worshipping the Golden Calf and realized that they were not ready for esoteric knowledge. However, the original interpretation of the Ten Commandments was still taught and under-stood via the kabbalistic oral tradition down the centuries and can be seen clearly by the kabbalist in the ten sefirot of the Tree of Life.

The Dalai Lama has said that we, as humans, need to know the laws of the universe well, so that we know which ones we can break. Conventional Judaism teaches that all other 613 laws (as listed in the books of Leviticus and Deuteronomy) can (and should) be overruled if someone's life is at stake – which is a similar assessment. If someone's life depends on telling an untruth, then placing the Ten Commandments on the Tree demonstrates that Hesed is further up the Tree than Tiferet and, used together with Judgement (Gevurah), Loving Kindness is greater even than Truth. In that case, the higher law super-sedes the lower law.

Moses destroyed the first command-ments when his followers demonstrated that they were not ready to receive or understand them.

THE TEN COMMANDMENTS

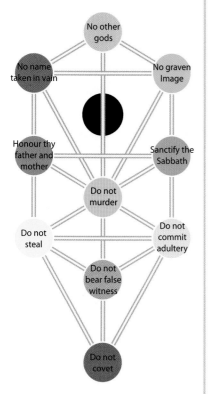

It is interesting to observe, however, that if we break one commandment, we quite frequently end up breaking them all. They are all essentially about learning not to betray ourselves, as much as others. If we steal, then we have coveted something that belongs to another. By stealing we have become a false witness to our true self and, by doing that, we are in danger of destroying some part of ourselves ... and so on.

Here are the Ten Commandments with a kabbalistic interpretation (see below). The first three are about our relationship with God. The commandments below the supernal triad of Binah/Keter/Hokhmah – across the divide of Da'at – are about our emotional and physical lives.

KETER: I am the Lord thy God; thou shalt have no other gods before me

It is important to note that this commandment does not say that there *are* no other gods. The Hebrew word used for 'gods' here is *Elohim*, which can be translated as many gods, rulers, judges, angels. It is saying I AM is God – the Keter of Keters – and it is greater than the Elohim that is placed at Hokhmah. To a kabbalist it means 'Go to the top, embrace the whole'. In this relative universe, the Keter of Keters is all that we can possibly imagine when it comes to God – and to worship any of the other aspects below that is going to put us out of balance.

Nowadays we have many more lesser gods: celebrities, fame itself, sport, money, business, sex. If we put them before our path in life, we may have a great time for a while but, sooner or later, we are going to stumble. The esoteric meaning is also to remember that I AM THAT I AM means acknowledging the God in ourselves and honouring that.

HOKHMAH: Thou shalt not make unto thee any graven image

This sefirah is traditionally associated with Adam as the first of the masculine principles – the Great Father. Kabbalistically it is a simple follow-on to commandment number one in that, if we make an image of what we think God might be, we are immediately limiting it and therefore we are quite likely to get the wrong idea.

The idea of Adam is to remind us of Adam Kadmon – the perfected human. To work to anything other than that goal is to create a graven image. We do not make Adam – or any other human being – God; we work to become like God ourselves.

The Jewish faith forbids depictions of God for this very reason. Michelangelo's painting on the roof of the Sistine Chapel where God and Adam are depicted together, and the works of many Renaissance masters and of the great poet William Blake, may have inspired Christians, but it could be said that they have perpetuated an image – and a very limiting image – of what God might be: that ubiquitous old man in the sky.

Kabbalah teaches that listening to the words of priests instead of investigating for ourselves is also a graven image, rather than true religion. The Koran (17: 36) backs this up: 'You shall not accept any information, unless you verify it for yourself. I have given you the hearing, the eyesight and the brain, and you are responsible for using them.'

It is also a graven image to represent ourselves as we are not. To call ourselves inferior, poor or unhappy is not an accurate image of God – and we are made in that image of abundance and truth. To think anything else is contrary to law and creates exactly what we do not want in our lives.

BINAH: Thou shalt not take the name of the lord thy God in vain

Binah is the first feminine principle and the place of Eve – the Great Mother.

Kabbalah teaches that this commandment is not actually about not saying, 'Oh my God!' when we are surprised – or if it is, that is a pretty small matter. It is more about not using the name of God to pray for worthless things: not invoking God to create things that are inappropriate for us or for others. The Hebrew word for 'take' is *nacah*, which also means 'lift up', so the commandment is not to lift up the name of God for dishonest or empty means.

So, don't pray if you don't really mean it! Don't go to the synagogue or church only for form's sake. Don't allow yourself to mouth the sacred words when you don't mean them.

HESED: Honour the Sabbath and keep it holy

The idea of the Sabbath is to create separation between work, and some space for ourselves. It is supposed to be devoted to worship and rest; a chance to recharge our batteries and an opportunity to remember our sacred origins, rather than a day of boredom imposed on us from above. As Jesus said (Mark 2: 27): 'The Sabbath was made for mankind, and not mankind for the Sabbath.'

A kabbalist would say that this Sabbath does not have to be on a specific day of the week, no matter that Islam states Friday, Judaism states Saturday and Christianity states Sunday. It is just about taking a 'Holy-day' once a week.

For anyone on a spiritual path, it is important to look for the truth over and above tribal belief.

This is a day for refocusing on ourselves and on our sacred link to the Divine; a time to give up – as in 'let go of' – everyday cares and work; a time to assess our life and relax in preparation for the next week's challenges. As this is an Hesedic principle, it is about the love of God and taking time to focus on that, rather than on the everyday hustle and bustle of life. The Hesedic principle is love and that includes love and respect for the self.

GEVURAH: Honour thy father and mother

Kabbalistically, honouring our father and mother has a wider brief than simply respecting our parents; it refers to honouring the tradition into which we were born. Many people who seek the Truth embark on what the great mystic Joseph Campbell called the 'Hero's Journey'. For anyone on a spiritual path, it is important to look for the truth over and above tribal belief. This may even mean adopting a different faith, but the ultimate goal is to use our journey to rediscover – and make peace with – the inner knowledge of our original tradition, as opposed to its outer trappings.

This commandment is also about honouring both the masculine and feminine aspects within any tradition.

TIFERET: Thou shalt not commit murder

This commandment is generally translated as 'Thou shalt not kill'. This comes from the Latin version of the Bible, known as the Vulgate, which dates from the end of the fourth century when Pope Damascus commissioned a new version of the Gospels from St Jerome. St Jerome's version, drawn from old Latin and Greek manuscripts, differed from earlier translations in that it interpreted the Hebrew word *ratsach* as 'kill', rather than as what kabbalists and Hebrew scholars believe to be the more accurate term 'murder'. Most Christian translations since then have borrowed from the Vulgate. The words *muwth* or *nakah*, which appear elsewhere in the Old Testament, are more accurately translated as 'kill'.

To murder means not only to kill physically with premeditation; it means to destroy someone's reputation, hopes, ambitions or faith (including our own). It is murder of our true self to follow the crowd when we know that our destiny lies elsewhere. To kill in self-defence is not murder.

Tiferet is the point where people wake up to life and reality – stepping out of the everyday world and leaving the tribe, society and family conditioning behind. Often spiritual work is derided and disliked because it does just that – changes people so that they no longer fit the mould.

NEZACH: Thou shalt not commit adultery

To a kabbalist, committing adultery means mixing together two things that do not match and that provoke an unhelpful reaction in each other. This can, of course, refer to sexual adultery, but as the biblical patriarchs often had more than one wife, it is open to a much wider brief. Sometimes remaining in a marriage that is not working can be as adulterous as being unfaithful to our partner.

It can also be a form of adultery to work for someone we hate, or even to spend Christmas with our family if it makes us grit our teeth and everyone has to pretend that all is well when it clearly is not.

HOD: Thou shalt not steal

To steal means to take away a reputation – or even a life – just as much as somebody else's property. We can steal other people's ideas and their kudos, by not acknowledging that they originated something that we are using. Kabbalistically, to steal something is an expression of belief in a lack in our own life. It is also stealing from ourselves and our own lives if we do not allow ourselves to develop fully as individuals. We can also steal other people's lives by making them serve us or stay with us when they do not wish to do so.

YESOD: Thou shalt not bear false witness

Kabbalists are taught that 'bearing false witness' does not simply mean telling lies; it can also mean misrepresenting ourselves or others in any way. In addition, it could mean telling the truth in a way that hurts others.

MALKHUT: Thou shalt not covet

This commandment is a very physical one: all about possession. Jesus' most remembered teachings about rich people turn on the matter of whether or not they can give up physical possessions when necessary. At no point does Jesus teach that we cannot be prosperous – or even rich; but he does teach that physical possessions can weigh us down if they become too important. It is also true that we cannot take them with us into the other worlds; they only belong in Assiyah. Likewise, the desire for things that belong to others will weigh us down – and will stop us from seeing the good in our own life.

The way to turn this commandment round is to realize that we are entitled to anything as good as our neighbour – but that by coveting what they have, instead of looking for the version that will serve *us*, we are blocking our divine likelihood of getting it.

To steal means to take away a reputation – or even a life – just as much as somebody else's property.

Simple changes, such as holding your toothbrush with a different grip, can feel strange at first but they teach your Yesod to feel more at ease with new and unfamiliar sensations.

Exercise
Learning to accept change

It is interesting to work out just how much of your life is run on automatic. When we are trying to 'wake up' to the truth, it often feels odd and even wrong to do so.

Try the following changes in your life and see how much your Yesod resists just these little things:

○ Sleep on the other side of the bed.
○ Brush your teeth in different order.
○ Cross your arms the other way.
○ Put your underwear on in a different order (e.g. left sock first instead of right).
○ Notice which foot you put forwards first each time you walk – and change it.
○ Use a different word to say 'hello' or 'goodbye' to people.
○ Promise yourself that you will meditate for five minutes each morning – and see how soon it is that you forget or find a good reason not to do it.

Exercise
Letting go of 'should'

It is a useful kabbalistic exercise to do absolutely nothing that you 'should' do for a whole day. Instead, give all your plans and expected behaviours more lee-way and let them flow naturally.

Obviously you may need to try this exercise when you have a day out of the office, since there are so many 'shoulds' in working life that it is difficult to avoid them. Using this exercise frees you up to understand what you truly think and feel about life, rather than going through it in automatic resentment at having to do things you do not want to do.

Exercise

Finding out who you are

This is an exercise to help you find out who you are (as opposed to who you think you are).

- ○ Make a list of ten of your greatest likes and dislikes.
- ○ Sit in quiet contemplation or meditation for ten minutes, then look again at your list. Consider it carefully while assessing *why* these are your likes and dislikes. Some of the contents of the list may still be accurate, but you may be surprised by how many you will discard at the end of the exercise.

If you repeat this exercise each day for a week you will become far more aware of who you truly are.

Exercise

What are your goals in life?

Write yourself a three-paragraph obituary which would be appropriate if you were to die tomorrow.

Then write the obituary you would truly like to have. Allow yourself everything you truly want – wealth, love, happiness and success.

Now make a list of the key points of the life you would like to have and make a commitment to do something every day which will bring them closer to you. These can be very simple things like buying a wedding magazine if you want to get married or visiting a place where wealthy people hang out if you want to be rich. Even simpler, just start talking to friends about who you want to be and what you would like to do with your life.

This will begin to retrain your Yesod to look for the things in life that you truly want rather than focusing on what you don't want and don't have. Whatever Yesod focuses on becomes reality for us.

Writing out our likes and dislikes or what we see as the truth about ourselves can be very revealing.

KABBALAH
and prosperity

Prosperity is the ability to create abundance in all areas of life, including health, relationships and finances. Spiritual people often resist the idea of working with prosperity consciousness because it brings up deep issues of self worth.

It is just as appropriate to use kabbalistic principles in our finances or love life as it is in our spiritual self-development.

Traditionally, Kabbalah was taught only to Jewish men over the age of 40 who already had a family, so that by the time they began studying this line of spiritual work, they would have demonstrated their maturity in coping with the everyday pressures of life, such as paying the rent and handling financial and relationship issues. However, Kabbalah can be a useful tool in helping us solve any financial or relationship problem. It is a discipline that is meant to work at every level, so it is just as appropriate to use kabbalistic principles in our finances or love life as it is in our spiritual self-development. After all, if we are constantly worried about money or relationships, much valuable time and energy will be spent on those situations, leaving little for spiritual work.

What PROSPERITY really is

Kabbalah teaches that if we are in alignment, then the universe will work for us. Kabbalistic prosperity is about working out where our thoughts and attitudes towards money are preventing us from being able to receive the natural abundance of the universe.

The first thing the kabbalist needs to understand about money is that it is a neutral energy form – and nothing else. It is an energetic symbol that humankind adopted in order to barter and create trade. As a form of energy, prosperity cannot be created or destroyed (the laws of physics state), but only changed and moved. Therefore burning a banknote is simply destroying a symbol of money; it does nothing to the source of the energy itself.

Money obeys the law of cause and effect just as everything else on Earth does. What we put out, we get back. So, if our consistent thoughts about money are that we have to work hard to get it, and that there is never enough to go round, that is the picture that will be reflected back to us. Fortunately, with a little will-power this can be changed.

Prosperity is not just about money. However, our attitudes towards abundance and lack – as represented by money – affect every other aspect of our life. Wealth is represented by the right-hand pillar of the Tree of Life and lack by the left-hand pillar. The right-hand pillar can over-balance in greed and possessiveness, while the left-hand one can revel in the 'pureness of poverty' or can punish us for not being 'good enough'.

However, through positive use of the left-hand pillar we can clear space for prosperity, and through positive use of the right-hand pillar we can initiate actions to create prosperity. The central pillar of consciousness is about drawing the prosperity down from God into the physical world. Held in balance on the central column of consciousness, we can always have quite enough to enjoy life as a prosperous and free spirit.

The Tree of Life is also known as the Tree of Abundance.

Money is neither good nor evil. It is purely an energy which obeys the universal law of cause and effect.

Common errors concerning PROSPERITY

There are ten basic kabbalistic reasons why people have money issues. The word for 'sin' in New Testament Greek is *hamartia*, which means 'to miss the mark' or 'to wander from the Law of God'. The word 'sin' is also said to be a medieval English archery term meaning 'to miss the mark'. So when we 'sin' we are putting ourselves out of alignment with our Divine Good. The most common errors we make with regard to prosperity are easily aligned with the ten sefirot of the Tree of Life:

○ KETER: Emotional or mental issues with religion, faith or the idea of God, which are projected onto money; also the fear of being thought 'unspiritual' if we are prosperous.

○ HOKHMAH: An inability to think laterally or an inability to be innovative in financial affairs.

Money is an energy that needs to flow and circulate to be healthy just like water or the blood in our bodies.

○ **BINAH:** Lack of understanding of universal law with regard to the way money works.

○ **HESED:** Lack of generosity to self and others.

○ **GEVURAH:** Living a cluttered life – leaving no space for the new.

○ **TIFERET:** Forgetting to be happy with the abundance already around and within us.

○ **NEZACH:** Lack of spiritual, emotional and mental action to create prosperity.

○ **HOD:** Avoidance of monitoring our financial situation.

○ **YESOD:** Fear of envy by others – or of being seen to be 'above ourselves'.

○ **MALKHUT:** The belief that 'there is never enough to go around'.

WATCHING our unconscious language

Money is a living energy. It needs to flow constantly, like the water in a river, in order to bring life and health to its surroundings. Thoughts, words, feelings, an overload of physical possessions – all these things can block the natural flow of abundance in our life.

First, we must never underestimate the power of words. How we speak about money affects what comes to us and what does not. Kabbalah teaches that the law of cause and effect takes things literally, and the majority of catch-phrases that we use today about money are negative. Even the most casual phrases have an effect without our knowing it. Over ten or 20 years of thoughtless repetition they can carry a great deal of power.

LETTING GO of guilt over money

Worrying about money not only stops us from developing our full potential, but makes us doubt the goodness of all things and can promote a vicious circle of unhappiness and lack.

Frequently, there is also guilt at the idea of being wealthy when there are so many poor and starving people in the world. But consider: how does it help others who are in trouble if we are not willing to prosper? Empathy will not help them. How can we possibly help the poor and starving if we are poor and starving ourselves? It is those people who are sufficiently wealthy to give who can offer the most help to those in need – not only in gifts, but in teaching others how they too may prosper. By understanding and applying the spiritual laws of prosperity we can help to spread much-needed abundance throughout the world.

Many people feel guilty about having money because they believe that spirituality and poverty go hand-in-hand, but a more careful reading of the Bible reveals that it is the will of God for Its children to enjoy abundance. It is made clear that having more than we need is not necessarily a good thing, but nowhere does the Bible endorse poverty as a spiritual goal. The quotation about money and evil, as written by St Paul (1 Timothy 6: 10), reads: 'the *love of money* is the root of all evil' and not 'money is the root of all evil'. This means that avarice (or going after money for its own sake) is not a good thing; it is not a comment on money itself.

People also tend to forget that Jesus of Nazareth said many positive things about prosperity. His 'negative teachings' include the well-known phrase: 'It is easier for a camel to pass through the eye of a needle than for a rich man to enter the Kingdom of Heaven' (Matthew 19: 24). Historians say that the 'eye of the needle' was the narrowest of the gateways into the city of Jerusalem and that any extra load had to be taken off a camel's back in order for the beast to pass through. Kabbalistically, this simply means that 'you can't take it with you' – that it is the attachment to wealth (the illusion that we cannot exist without it) that is the problem, rather than wealth itself.

Jesus paid his taxes and his dues; he had wonderful meals and banquets with friends; he was capable of bringing in huge shoals of fish to sell in order to benefit his disciples. Biblical scholars will confirm that he did not have the slightest problem with abundance. What he did warn against was the temptation to let wealth and possessions get in the way of a spiritual life.

A simple, workable PROSPERITY plan

Applying the aspects of the ten sefirot of the Tree of Life positively to our financial beliefs and actions gives us enough information to begin to experience lasting prosperity. Some sefirot will not be a problem; others may represent major challenges. However, applying just some of the suggestions given below should make the financial situation improve. The good news is that prosperity work has a knock-on effect on the rest of our lives.

KETER: Acknowledge the higher source

Money, like everything else in this world, comes from God. God is the source of our supply and, if we are not abundant, it is all too easy to blame God or to believe that It does not want us to be rich, rather than to see the inner resistance that is blocking our good.

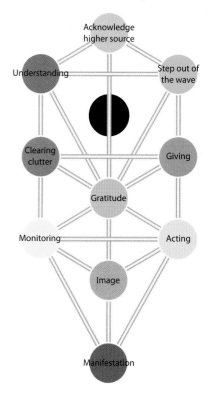

THE TREE OF PROSPERITY

Acknowledge higher source

Understanding

Step out of the wave

Clearing clutter

Giving

Gratitude

Monitoring

Acting

Image

Manifestation

Kabblah teaches that God loves us all. You can be a multi-millionaire or live on the streets and God will love you equally.

A God that allows us choice in everything is constantly offering us good options as well as bad. Align ourselves with the Law, and good will come; disobey the Law, and we become uncomfortable. Subconsciously we may believe that God did not invent money, so it cannot have anything to do with God. But money is energy – which comes from God – and we humans decided to use this energy to make things fair rather than unfair.

For example, one man has a pig and another has chickens. They trade: a haunch of the pig for a year's supply of eggs. One year the pig dies, but the first man still needs the eggs, so he offers a token to promise that next year he will give two haunches of pig instead of the usual one, as long as he can still have the eggs. That is all that money is: an agreement of trade between two people.

Our fear over money works in the same way that we fear God. We think we will get shouted at for letting the pig die in the first place; then, when we have continued to receive the eggs for an extra year, we resent giving the second haunch of pig. If we fear God and do not think we are worthy of Its love, then we will also fear money for exactly the same reason. Fear attracts exactly what is feared, so if we focus on lack we will create it; but if we focus on prosperity, we will create that instead.

When people leave conventional religion for the New Age, their finances often take a terrible tumble, because there is a deep inner belief that they cannot do what they love and prosper at the same time. This comes from the conviction that 'truly spiritual' people are poor, and that if we want to demonstrate that we are good, then we have to struggle. It's the hair-shirt and bread-and-water syndrome: beat yourself up physically and mentally, and live in the humiliation of not being able to pay the bills, and the soul will be cleansed.

Kabbalah teaches that God loves us all. You can be a multi-millionaire or live on the streets and God will love you equally. Whoever and whatever you are, you are a vital component in God's cosmic plan. Without you, the plan would fail, so you are infinitely precious to God. God is constantly offering abundance with every breath you take. If you cannot see that – and you want to do so – then you need to think laterally. And that is where Hokhmah comes in.

HOKHMAH: Step out of line

We can create revolution through revelation! We live in a world of bad news, soap operas, grumbling, gossip and television celebrities. None of that is real, but the more attention we give it, the more destructive it becomes. So why do we avidly watch other people's distress? What are we creating by default when we do? Most genuinely 'bad news', such as the death of someone we love, is incredibly private and needs to be addressed in peace and safety.

Negativity is catching. It is common practice to be cross when a utilities bill arrives and needs to be paid – but the truth is that we have been given all of that power on credit because the utilities company trusts us to be prosperous enough to pay. They have faith in us.

To prosper, change the energy. Thank the power company for supplying you. Bless the cheque you write to pay them. Stop reading the paper and watching the news whenever possible; avoid soap operas that are full of angst and watch movies with happy endings. Choose how *you* want to live your life, instead of letting the outside world live it for you.

The choice is ours: we can live life consciously and make positive decisions based on free will, which will draw good times towards us – or we can live life by default, and be drawn into the culture of fear and negativity that predominates around us.

BINAH: Understand how you got here

The odds are that you got where you are now through living life by default – and by believing what your religious tradition, your parents and your teachers taught you.

Understanding comes when we realize that the universe is totally neutral and that if we bemoan our poverty, lack of relationships, boredom and irritation, cosmic law will simply assume that – as we are focusing our attention on these things – we want more of them. And it will readily hand out more.

It is important to look at the religious training we may have received about money and wealth. Rereading holy texts, such as the Old and New Testaments in the Bible, can teach us many prosperity secrets. For example, Moses and the Israelites of the Exodus had treasure given to them by the people of Egypt when they left. This treasure built the Tabernacle, which was later transformed into the inner sanctum of the Jewish Temple. They also received manna from Heaven: everything they needed every day of their lives on the way to the Promised Land – and that is the secret of true prosperity.

Buddha renounced the riches inherent in being a prince, but they were mere clutter to him – not true abundance. He did not become poor, for he chose the middle path, having tried both the ascetic life of self-denial and the life of riches and royalty. Mohammed was inundated by people giving him riches and houses.

Be careful how much time you give to absorbing negative images and ideas from newspapers, TV and radio.

If you pay the bills and neglect yourself, that good old cosmic law kicks in and just thinks you want bills and debts to be more important than you are.

It is always worth investigating the inner truths of all religions. They usually tell us to take only as much as we need – and that means enough to pay our bills and to live peacefully so that we are able to be happy and to grow. It does not mean that we have to be poor.

HESED: Giving

Many people in spiritual work are good givers and poor receivers. However, the great spiritual disciplines of the world suggest quite a different kind of giving from the one we generally understand. In kabbalistic teaching there are three levels of giving (in the Bible these are known as 'tithing'). They go in this order:

○ Give to God
○ Give to yourself for celebration
○ Give to others

Most people work in a different order: they give to other people first and foremost, to themselves next and to God (or their spiritual growth) last. Some people go even further and refuse to give to themselves at all. This results in cosmic law doing the same to them.

How do you give to God? The old way was to give to the Temple because that donation paid the priests, whose job was to remind the Israelites of the wonders of the oral teaching; one gave as a thank-offering to God for guidance in how to live life. Today people who 'tithe' give their money to their sources of spiritual inspiration – whether this is a church, a group or an individual person. It is important to ensure that this tithe is not charity – that it is not given to support good works, but as an acknowledgement of inspiration received.

Tithing is popular in the United States where many of the big corporations were founded by families that tithed regularly. These included the Kraft, Colgate, Heinz and Rockefeller families, all of whom have spoken publicly of their belief that putting God first financially prospered their business. When people criticized his wealth, John D. Rockefeller would say: 'God gave me my money' (*Open Your Mind to Receive* by Dr Catherine Ponder).

You can also give to God by putting your spiritual growth first. So, in order to prosper, it helps to ensure that you give yourself time and backing to be who you really want to be – before you take care of others. It is worth checking if you pay the bills *before* you buy yourself a bunch of flowers or a bottle of wine. If you pay the bills and neglect yourself, that good old cosmic law kicks in and just thinks you want bills and debts to be more important than you are – and so it keeps on giving you more of them. It is all about balance: don't neglect your obligations, but value yourself too. It can take a few months of practising this to change the tide, but it will happen.

GEVURAH: Clearing out clutter

The word 'possession' is an interesting one. Do you possess your possessions, or do they possess you? If your happiness depends on physical objects, then it may lead to financial, emotional and even physical problems. The balance is about having beautiful things in your life that you can let go of any time you need to do so – rather than having your possessions owning you and cluttering your life. You can also have a cluttered mind, to the extent of focusing on a particular belief that is addictive and exclusive (a form of psychological possession).

Jesus of Nazareth was an itinerant preacher, wise enough in the laws of prosperity to know that everywhere he went he would be taken care of, fed and offered a bed for the night. He could manifest whatever he wanted wherever he was (including the money to pay his taxes); he was a Master and those who followed him were in training to be the same. They could not simply stay in one place or carry all their possessions with them.

Nowadays clutter-clearing is all the rage and people realize that holding on to old pictures, letters, ornaments and so on means that they are also holding on to the attached emotions. It may not be tactful to throw out the vase that Auntie June gave you, but if every time you see it you think how much you dislike it – or her – then it is not doing either of you any good and should be discarded.

It is important to be kind to yourself while you clear out your possessions; some people do it in one fell swoop, while others need to do it slowly and gently. Get a good friend to help; they will be more dispassionate than you about what needs to go and what does not.

TIFERET: Gratitude

The Tiferet 'secret' is to look for beauty – where you find that, you will also find truth. Yesod often tries to persuade us that the world is a bad place but Tiferet knows that it is not so. The poet John Keats summed it up in his 'Ode on a Grecian Urn':

○ Beauty is truth, truth beauty – that is all
   Ye know on earth, and all ye need to know.

Having the discipline to keep your home clean and clear of rubbish is a good way of keeping the clutter down.

You will get better prosperity results from eating just one course at a four-star restaurant than you will by going to a fast-food restaurant a dozen times.

The best way to find beauty is to acknowledge everything good that we already have and are – this helps us to find our true self. Being grateful for what we have is a powerful way of applying cosmic law, even if the idea makes us wince because Grandma was always saying, 'Count your blessings, dear!'

First, it shows the universe that you are focusing your mind on the kind of things you truly want, as opposed to things you *don't* want. Second, it helps you remember yourself – or put yourself back together when you are in pieces. Third, it helps you to work out what in your life you *don't* want to focus on any more.

HOD: Monitoring your progress

It is very easy to let your finances slip through your fingers through lack of attention. Make sure that you check your bank statements; read the meter instead of relying on estimates; find out if you can have a free financial review from your bank.

Make sure that you aren't paying standing orders or direct debits that are out of date; check that all your due payments come in and that you do not pay too much tax. Make sure you keep in good communication with people over financial matters: tell the bank ahead of time if you are likely to go overdrawn.

Keep a journal of your prosperity work; have a 'gratitudes book' in which you can write your thanks for every day; and make an 'elimination list' of things you want the universe to remove from your life. You may make some interesting discoveries.

Work out exactly what you would spend a large amount of money or a windfall on. If you do not know why you want that money, it is hard for cosmic law to arrange for you to win the lottery. Unless you are a natural accountant monitoring your finances may be the place of greatest resistance for the Yesodic ego. It requires discipline and, if that is lacking, other areas are almost certainly out of balance.

YESOD: Cleaning up your image

We live in a world where everyday life is ruled by Yesod, and the Law works for personal appearance just as much as for whatever lies in your heart. It notes what you wear and where you pass your time. The choice is up to you, but you will get better prosperity results from eating just one course at a four-star restaurant than you will by going to a fast-food restaurant a dozen times. If you want abundance, you have to align yourself with it so that the universe agrees that it is where you belong.

As Ernest Bramah says in *The Wallet of Kai Lung*, 'It is a mark of insincerity of purpose to spend one's time in looking for the sacred Emperor in the low-class tea-rooms.' So go where your purpose is. If you feel broke, but you want to mark a special occasion, choose brunch at a good hotel rather than dinner at a place that does not inspire you.

Wear clothes that are smart (whatever the fashion). It is true that one good-quality suit and two well-made shirts are worth a dozen cheap, fashionable outfits. If you are into New Age philosophy, then consider carefully the image that you put out. Be aware that to others you may just look impoverished or weird, rather than wise and spiritual, if you wear bright, floaty dresses or cheesecloth shirts.

The everyday world's Yesod makes snap judgements, whether we like it or not. The task of the kabbalist is to be 'in the world but not of it', and that means fitting in where necessary – for instance, if you want to get that job. You are not compromising yourself; you are accepting what is and agreeing to work with it. You can attempt to change things, if you want to, once you are inside. It is not about trying to make yourself something you are not, or showing off or being vain; but about revealing your true value to the world in a way that it can be observed by others.

Another thing that may be blocking your prosperity at the level of Yesod is your attitude to those who are already prosperous. Do you envy rich people? What do you think other people would think of you if you were rich? Do you think some people have no right to wealth, or that they misuse it? Do you snarl when you see someone in an expensive car? Or feel jealous when you see somebody who, in your opinion, has very little talent, but is paraded all over a magazine showing off their wealth? Do you refer to 'fat cats' when you read about rich businessmen and women?

If so, you are likely to push your own prosperity away because you are demonstrating a subconscious belief that you, too, would be envied or disliked for being rich. What goes around comes around, and your feelings towards others will reflect back on you. That is a good reason for not becoming wealthy.

It may be that you would use riches in a better way than other people. But remember, you do not know the full story of their wealth. Quit judging others as soon as you can and allow them to be happy in their prosperity. Then you too have a greater chance of being admired rather than despised when you too are wealthy. A good way to transform this energy is to observe the rich and famous and say to yourself quietly, 'Good for you. And it's good for me, too.'

What goes around comes around, and your feelings towards others will reflect back on you.

In order for people to give with joy, others have to be willing to receive with joy.

MALKHUT: Receiving

Most of us think that receiving should be the easy part. 'Just watch me spend my lottery winnings!' you might say. But you might be surprised how much subconscious resistance has been trained into you when it comes to receiving.

Take a look at your everyday attitudes. If someone gives you a compliment, what is your reaction? If they say they like your outfit, do you say, 'Oh this old thing!' If they say you look good, do you say you feel lousy? If they say they admire you, do you make a face and a self-deprecating remark? Cosmic law hears you – and will acknowledge that you do not want to receive compliments; therefore, logically, you will not want to receive anything else.

Take a good look at how you receive what you are given physically, too. Will you let someone else buy you a cup of coffee at the office without insisting on giving them the money every time? Even more, will you let them get you a coffee – or are you always getting the coffee for everyone else? When someone you really like gives you a present, do you ever say, 'You shouldn't have'? Why shouldn't they have? They wanted to make you happy.

Not receiving anything, whether it is a compliment or a gift, is to deny the person who gives it to you the opportunity of giving. That is really quite unkind. Why should you be the only one who always has the blessing of being the giver? To be a giver, someone has to receive. Maybe it is your turn.

Likewise, to deny the truth of what other people are saying is to deny them. You are effectively telling them that their opinion is valueless, if they think you are good-looking and you tell them that you are not. They have the right to have you respect their opinion. If you genuinely believe that they are telling a lie – then call their bluff. You can still receive the compliment; the rest is their problem for trying to deceive you.

The whole secret to kabbalistic prosperity is to realize that the issue is between God and ourselves; nobody else. God is the active, giving principle when it comes to energy; it is up to us humans to select and receive the amounts and types of energy that we want. Using our knowledge of the Tree of Life, we can do just that.

Exercise

Checking your language

What are your favourite phrases about money? What did your parents always say about it? An important aspect in understanding your relationship with money is identifying the loading that you received from your parents. Are they prosperous? What is their attitude towards rich people? Did they ever refer to people 'getting above themselves'? Or are they well off, and you want to rebel against them and their lifestyle to punish them? Your parents' beliefs will have gone deep into your subconscious, even if they were only meant to be throw-away lines. (Of course some people will have a positive loading from their parents and family – it does not all have to be bad.) Try and observe the comments about money that you yourself make on an everyday basis. Some of the most common negative phrases are:

- ○ Money can't buy you love
- ○ Money is the root of all evil
- ○ Poor little rich girl
- ○ Neither for love nor money
- ○ Money doesn't grow on trees

To turn the tide, stop using these phrases and try never again to express a negative feeling about money. It will take time, conscious thought and discipline, but it will be worth it.

Exercise:

Showing gratitude

If you want fast results, write out 100 things you are grateful for, every night for a week. They may be the same things each night or different ones, or a mixture of the two. To make it easier, you can start with the five senses. Try saying 'thank you' for:

- ○ Ten things you enjoy looking at
- ○ Ten things you enjoy listening to
- ○ Ten things you enjoy touching or feeling
- ○ Ten things you like to eat
- ○ Ten lovely scents

Your gratitude can be for things as small and simple as you like – even a cup of tea or the sight of sunshine on leaves.

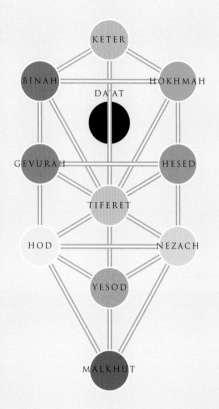

Exercise
Making a prosperity wheel

Kick-starting prosperity takes action. Affirmations are useful – they are positive statements in the present tense that inform and instruct the universe what we want in life. Instead of saying, 'I haven't enough', try affirming, 'My income is constantly increasing and I prosper wherever I turn.' It may not be true when you start, but it can become true if you pay it enough attention. A wonderful Nezachian way to start changing negative prosperity into positive abundance is to create a prosperity wheel.

○ Take a large piece of coloured card (green or gold works best for finances; pink for love; and blue or white for intellectual/educational desires) and put a smiling picture of you in the centre, at Tiferet.

○ Then surround yourself with coloured pictures of whatever you want to bring into your life – or whatever you want to maintain or develop – and add the spokes of the wheel to draw the experiences to you. To apply kabbalistic principles, places pictures of whatever you want at the appropriate levels around your own photo:

KETER: images of spirituality or place your affirmation here.
HOKHMAH: images of sources of inspiration and delight.
BINAH: images of understanding – books, The Bible, etc.
BINAH/GEVURAH: images of health, diet and exercise.
GEVURAH/HOD: images of the perfect job.
HOD: images of travel.
HOD/YESDOD/MALKHUT: images of money.
MALKHUT/YESOD/NEZACH: images of a beautiful home.
NEZACH: images of happy family and friends.
HESED/NEZACH: images of love and romance.

○ Put the wheel up on the wall and look at it morning and night.

○ You also need to add the 'universal disclaimer'. This is really important because it moves the intention to the realm of Grace, rather than just personal desire: 'These things or better now manifest for me in easy and pleasant ways for the highest good of all concerned.' This ensures that you draw to you abundance that is yours by divine right and take nothing away from others that belongs to them.

Two words of warning: the universe can be very literal in its interpretation of the Law, so take care what you ask for – you may get it. One woman put up a picture of herself holding her brother's baby son and asked for better family relationships, and she was pregnant within six months. And do not ask for things that are not your business, or which would cause hurt to others.

Universal disclaimer
'These things or better now manifest for me in easy and pleasant ways for the highest good of all concerned.'

SPIRIT

UNDERSTANDING

INSPIRATION

HEALTH

LOVE

WORK

HAPPY FAMILY
AND FRIENDS

TRAVEL

BEAUTIFUL
HOME

MONEY

KABBALAH
and relationships

Kabbalah is a teaching both understands duality and promotes unity. It would support the idea that beneath the surface of most of the world's problems lies a conflict between the masculine and feminine pillars of the Tree of Life.

These problems manifest in the world as an imbalance between giving and receiving and, in everyday life, between men and women.

In a world of duality, conflict has to exist – it is the way we deal with it that matters. For a seed to grow, it must break its shell, push against the earth and be stronger than the plants around it that might block it from the sun. What goes 'wrong' with humans is that unlike animals (which also fight for food, sex and survival), we find it hard to forgive, forget and move on once the battle has been won or lost.

The American cancer surgeon Bernie Siegel (author of *Love, Medicine and Miracles*) once said that the best thing that could happen to the human race would be for everyone to lose his or her memory each night at midnight. Then there would be no vendettas, wars or destructive memories.

This means that the only real issue to be dealt with in relationships of any kind is balance. The problem is duality: one side of it is masculine and the other feminine. Where there is trouble, this usually manifests as an imbalance between giving and receiving. One of us wants to give, but the other does not want to receive what the other is giving; one of us feels that the other is not giving enough; neither of us will give – or neither of us will receive. Any of these combinations can lead to feelings of resentment and guilt. Neither resentment nor guilt is an agent for change; they are traps that keep us locked up and that feed themselves over and over again. Ultimately, they lead to attack and defence – which means war.

Working out dynamics and archetypes

The sefirot represent the different archetypes (mental images chosen by the individual as he or she grows up) within us, as expressed by the Greek gods, the planets (see page 52) and Jungian psychology. We all have an image of our perfect animus (male archetype) and anima (female archetype), according to our astrology, upbringing, genes and favourite fairy tales. Subconsciously we look for them in our mate and in ourselves, often finding only bitter disappointment. Psychology teaches us that we search in our partner for the parts of ourselves that need healing from childhood. So we subconsciously choose people who are similar to our parents, to give ourselves another chance to address the same issues.

We all relate to some of these archetypes better than to others. Placing them on the Tree shows the interaction of the levels within us (see right).

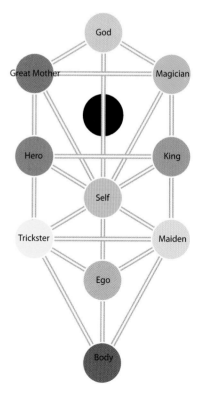

THE ARCHETYPES

- ○ MALKHUT is the Earth Mother – Gaia, Ceres or Demeter (Jung: the Body).
- ○ YESOD is the Moon goddess – Diana the huntress for the crescent Moon, and Artemis the many-breasted goddess for the full Moon (Jung: the Ego).
- ○ HOD is the young man who is into everything and has much information, but little knowledge – Mercury/Hermes (Jung: the Trickster).
- ○ NEZACH is the sexual woman – Aphrodite/Venus (Jung: the Maiden).
- ○ TIFERET is the Sun god Apollo/Helios, proud and powerful and sometimes beguiled by his own beauty (Jung: the Self/Guide/Wise Old Man).
- ○ GEVURAH is Mars/Ares or Athene, the strong and successful warrior, but with a fierce temper that can run out of control (Jung: the Hero).
- ○ HESED is Jupiter – jovial and kingly, but also capable of sexual excess, lack of control and overeating (Jung: the King).
- ○ BINAH is Chronos/Saturn, translated as the grandmother figure – Saturnine, wise and knowledgeable, but sometimes much too stern (Jung: the Great Mother).
- ○ HOKHMAH is the grandfather figure – Ouranos/Uranus, revelationary and fun, but sometimes so off-the wall that it could even be dangerous (Jung: the Magician).
- ○ KETER represents the Divine (God).

In addition to the archetypes, Kabbalah teaches that each sefirah defines a certain age of humanity and, according to the rest of our psychological make-up, we add our own psychological age and appropriate individual genders to each one:

- ○ MALKHUT babyhood
- ○ YESOD early childhood up to the age of seven
- ○ HOD school age – up to about 14
- ○ NEZACH puberty to marriage
- ○ TIFERET 20s and 30s; parents
- ○ GEVURAH early middle age
- ○ HESED late middle age
- ○ BINAH retirement and wisdom
- ○ HOKHMAH old age
- ○ KETER death and transformation

We all carry each archetype within us – and each level – and the way we feel within those ages, characteristics and sexualities can determine how we behave in a quarrel. For example, if someone is criticising you, which of them do you become? Are you angry (Gevurah) or offended (negative Tiferet pride)? Or do you feel like a child being told off (Hod, Yesod or Nezach)? In relationships, are you the fleet, elusive Moon goddess tempting and eluding an ever-more frustrated king? Are you the Earth Mother trying to nurture the grandfather who wants to be left alone to revel in inspiration? Are you the youth trying to outdo the warrior through trickery?

We take on different sex roles with specific people, according to how we feel most comfortable. One of us may be being Dad (male Tiferet or Hesed) to the other's child (feminine Hod), even though we are the same age and the same sex. We may both be playing either little girl or little boy. The man may be playing Mum as the woman plays son. We dance between the sefirot and the pillars, according to the way our psyches are made up.

If you always felt a little girl to your parents during every conflict, you are still likely to play the little girl with your boss or peers if they are angry. If you had to be Mum to your parents, because they were sick or weak, then you will probably try to be Mum to your colleagues and friends too. If your partner is playing the child, you can make the conflict balanced by refusing to be the Mum or Dad. Once you have noticed what is going on (from Tiferet, the place of the true self) you can even assume the same role as they are, if you like, and have a tantrum! Changing the energy in any argument will often kick the other person into Tiferet too, because it is different and unusual, and Yesod will not know what to do.

Venus is a Nezachian archetype. This painting of Venus is sexuality personified and not afraid to show it.

MASCULINE versus FEMININE

Kabbalah teaches that all souls have a leaning towards one particular sex or the other. The purpose of reincarnation is to balance us out as perfect human beings and, if we grow too masculine as a man or too feminine as a woman over a series of lives, then we may be offered a successive incarnation as the opposite sex.

This can be a great challenge, especially to male souls who have been soldiers or leaders of men and then incarnate as women and are expected to be feminine. Equally, female souls who have relied on men to take care of them and who have never had to build a career (they might not have incarnated for a hundred years or so) can find it hard to come down as a man and have to make their way in the animal world of work.

Women, in particular, often find great relief in the realization that they have been more used to living life as a man. It explains why they have trouble with relationships or at work, and why they cannot understand their parents or life itself – everything feels as if they are going against the grain. Kabbalah would say that such a powerful woman is here to learn what it is like to be feminine. She can still be powerful and successful, but joy will come from using more of her feminine energy than her masculine and from allowing her partner – and others – to support her, instead of trying to be the boss at all times.

It can be much more difficult for a man to accept that he has lived many lives as a woman, because of all the negative stereotypes that have existed down the ages. However, his task is to be properly masculine instead of overly passive, despite the fact that it may feel uncomfortable to start with. Knowledge is power and, once the situation is understood, he can begin to respond differently to situations in his life.

In such cases, relationships are often the hardest challenge, with masculine women automatically linking up with feminine men (who are used to being courted, so will feel that this is natural). This situation can work if both partners are happy to carry out their past roles, with the woman as the dominant part-ner, but it frequently leads to resentment and a lack of fulfilment as both struggle with their contradictory natures.

A feminine soul incarnated as a man who marries a masculine soul incarnated as a woman will initially admire her as being everything that his animus wants to be; but then he may grow to hate her, because she either rules him or represents everything that he is not – and which she will not allow him to be.

Men and women often lack understanding of the masculine and feminine aspects of the Tree of Life within themselves.

In the same way, a masculine woman may come to despise a feminine man because she can outrun and outfight him, even if only psychologically. It is even more destructive if he makes decisions to spite her and keep her down by manipulating her, instead of exerting masculine power, which she will recognize and respond to. This kind of action will generally be subconscious.

To a kabbalist, the answer would appear to be for a masculine woman to link up with another masculine soul who is incarnated as a man. They may have some scuffles, but man/man will generally outrun woman/man and the cross-soul woman will get to carry out her destiny as the female, while respecting her partner as more powerful than she. Likewise, the feminine man will work out his destiny best with a female/female, who will allow him to grow into his manhood and not fight him every step of the way.

It is not about being the greater or the lesser; it is about a dance of partnership that supports both souls in their joy and growth.

How to redress the BALANCE

It helps to look at *where* all the levels of conflict between masculine and feminine stand on the Tree and to assess our own strengths and weaknesses. For this I am indebted to the work of the late Danaan Parry, founder of the Earthstewards' Network. Danaan worked in conflict resolution in high-profile trouble spots – with Catholics and Protestants in Belfast, and with Hindus and Muslims in India – and developed a structure for ten 'laws of conflict' that pinpoint the ways in which we can identify what is really going on and resolve it.

Danaan and his wife, Jerilyn Brusseau, also developed workshops called 'Essential Peacemaking – Men and Women', because they learnt that it was the conflict between male and female that fuelled the rest of the conflict in the world. Merging Danaan's teaching on conflict resolution with the Tree of Life gives a wonderful demonstration on how truth follows similar structures in different traditions (see left).

Danaan outlined ten rules of conflict, nine of which fit directly onto the Tree. The tenth, 'Be a Warrior of the Heart', is actually the title of his book on resolving conflict and, to the kabbalist, is a repetition of the Tiferet principle. To make the Tree complete, we need only add one extra component: 'Acknowledgement'; in Danaan's teaching, this was one of the primary tools always used, but was not set out as a specific rule.

In using these laws of conflict, a kabbalist can address all the problems and issues set out within our own personal archetypes.

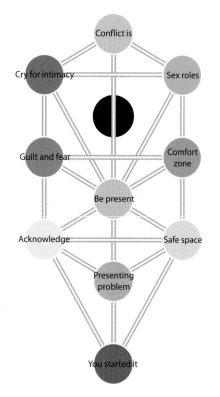

THE TREE OF CONFLICT

Conflict is

Cry for intimacy

Sex roles

Guilt and fear

Comfort zone

Be present

Acknowledge

Safe space

Presenting problem

You started it

KETER: conflict is

Kabbalistically, this represents the initial creation of a universe where duality would have to exist. The day that we are completely without conflict we will ascend from the Earth. Life is a continual state of growth and that cannot be done without conflict. However, that does not mean life needs to be painful, depressing, angry or competitive; it means that there is always conflict around us that will touch us. Whether it is conflict in the Middle East, a feeling of discomfort over our relationship with our mother-in-law, or an irritation with our partner over the washing up, it is how we react to conflict that is important. We can choose to ignore it, be angry with it, or deal with it and pass on. God invented conflict – it is part of the deal.

HOKHMAH: sex roles are always a part of conflict

As Hokhmah represents the first separation into masculine and feminine principles – the creation of active and passive principles – and as one side of the Tree is out of balance without the other, there has to be conflict between the sexes. Hokhmah is the 'Great Father' (either inspirational and revelatory or a bully). Our own kabbalistic make-up will determine whether we use the masculine or feminine energies best, but it is important to realize that gender conflict is there – and that a male partner can even be acting as 'Mummy' or 'little girl,' and vice versa. Once we can see that, we have already stepped away from the problem and will be able to observe it with greater clarity.

BINAH: conflict is a cry for intimacy

Binah is the first step in trying to recreate unity. Binah works best in partnership with Hokhmah, balancing the Tree. The dynamic of the relationship is vital at all points.

We cannot have a conflict without a relationship. Wherever there is disagreement it is because of differing opinions, and we are having a relationship with someone with whom we disagree just as much as we are with someone whom we like. Resolution of conflict always deepens the relationship.

Even more importantly, conflict is always a cry for intimacy. If we can understand that there are only two ways of operating – giving love and asking for love – then it becomes obvious that any anger thrown is a plea for understanding and love. Conflict resolution is not about problem solving; once one problem goes, another may come. It is about resolving the need between people to create problems.

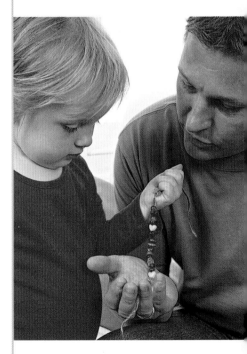

Our roles within relationships change constantly. If this father hurt himself, his daughter might well become 'Mum' for a few minutes in order to comfort him.

Once the truth is revealed, it is obvious that conflict is a cry for real contact and understanding between those involved.

Often it seems impossible to see that love is involved, but most of our quarrels depend on hiding what the upset is really about (see Yesod, page 96). Once the truth is revealed, it is obvious that conflict is a cry for real contact and understanding between those involved.

HESED: know your comfort zone

Hesed is the principle of Loving Kindness – and in conflict it is vital to love ourselves and do everything we can to be balanced and comfortable. If we do not, the conflict will automatically escalate through our discomfort.

Everyone needs a place of safety where they can curl up and recover or rest, and where no one else can reach them. Growth can be a tiring business and we all need our own personal comfort zone. It doesn't have to be a physical place. It can be a piece of music which relaxes us; an animal who accepts us unconditionally; or even a bar of chocolate. It is somewhere conflict does not intrude.

Change occurs only on the edge of that comfort zone. It does not happen within it because there is no conflict there. We need to be within reach of our place of security to feel strong enough to fight (when we need to fight) or surrender (when we need to surrender). If we are a long way from that zone there may be too much fear to react clearly to conflict. We must always make sure that we are near our secure haven or have access to whatever represents it, whenever there is recognizable conflict ahead.

GEVURAH: guilt and fear are not agents of change

The side triad of Hod/Gevurah/Tiferet is the place of guilt and fear – and the paralysis that characterizes them. Guilt and fear keep people enmeshed in situations. Imposing guilt and fear on others stops them growing and is not a way of resolving conflict.

People who feel guilty hide themselves and are ashamed. They do not come out of their comfort zones, therefore they cannot change. Those who impose guilt and fear are trying to take control of the situation. That means they have to keep topping up their control for the rest of their lives or face the breakdown of the world they are trying to create.

Today so many people live their lives in a haze of stress as they try to keep control of difficult situations. Helping the other person to relax and come away from the need to control is the only way that anything can be resolved for good.

TIFERET: be present at every moment

Tiferet is the pivotal point of the Tree of Life. Here, we are conscious. It is easy to try and run away from conflict mentally while we are in the middle of it. People sometimes just blank out or run previous arguments in their minds, instead of listening to what is being said *now*. There is no point in having last week's quarrel over and over again. We need to listen to what is being said before we can accept or reject it. We need to concentrate on what is going on behind the words. If we don't attend, we may miss a solution that is right in front of us.

NEZACH: create a safe space to heal conflict

Nezach is about action. To resolve conflict we often need to move; get up and walk around; even go outside. Otherwise we may stay stuck in negative energy. It is helpful to be on neutral ground to be able to heal conflict. Both protagonists should be away from their own territory. Meeting conflict in our own home or workplace or in their home or workplace puts added pressure on both sides. It is far easier to be rational and clear when both sides meet face-to-face in a safe space; away from all the holding energies that may exist at home we can think clearly. Partners will find it far easier to resolve problems if they go out for a walk together, for a meal or away for the day.

Safe emotional space between both parties is just as important. Perhaps an impartial third person with the role of conflict resolver (Tiferet) is necessary to help both sides get together and start to communicate without fear.

HOD: acknowledge what you see and hear

Hod is about communication – or trickery. Most breakdowns in communication arise from people refusing to listen to and acknowledge another's point of view; or, sometimes, from deliberately distorting what the other person has said. You do not have to agree with the other person's point of view, but a great deal will be achieved in any difficult situation through simple acknowledgement. 'I can see how upset you are. I understand that you are very angry and I'm sorry you feel so bad' is not giving ground – it is having the courtesy to accept that your partner has a different point of view and is experiencing pain because of it. Once you have listened to them and allowed them to express what they feel, they will find it much easier to listen to your point of view. It is even better to repeat their words back to them exactly as they were spoken, then they truly know that they have been heard and listened to. It is surprisingly hard to do.

YESOD: the presenting problem is never the real problem

Yesod is the foundation of the quarrel. It will usually be running its own patterns and defending itself and, if you can move to Tiferet and observe the disagreement, you will discover that whatever you or your partner is angry about is a cover-up for what is really going on. For example, you may think you are upset because one of you never clears up, or has forgotten an anniversary. But if you go deep within yourself, you may find that the root cause of the anger is unfinished business from a previous relationship (probably between you and one or both parents).

We get angry because we feel hurt, unloved, not good enough or threatened. Feeling upset because you are forgotten represents a classic self-fulfilment of a belief that you are not loved and appreciated. The real reason may sometimes be obscure, but you can always access it by asking yourself how old you feel when you experience the anger or pain. The answer will come back: 'three', 'six', 'twelve', and so on. Then ask yourself, 'What happened to me when I was that age?' and take deep, connected breaths as you go back in your mind. You will find the source of that anger.

MALKHUT: you started it!

No matter how unfair or irrational the conflict seems to be, the only thing you need to know about a fight is that you started it, just by existing and drawing it into your life – and only *you* can end it, by a change of attitude, by refusing to engage or by moving away. The law is that once you change, the other person will also change – they have to. But if you wait for them to change, you may well be in that particular conflict for the rest of your days – either with that person or with others.

The 'LAW OF CHANGE' and how it has to work

Because the sefirot of the Tree of Life are linked together by the paths, whatever happens to one sefirah will have a direct effect on all those connected to it. Therefore, if you change one aspect of your life, it will have a knock-on effect throughout the rest of it. What is even more amazing is that, if you change, others around you will change, too.

For example, take the idea of acknowledging what another person has to say in an argument, instead of automatically refuting it. You and your partner

Brooding over someone who has 'done us wrong' will not solve the issue. We need to find out what sparked that conflict in the first place.

may always be quarrelling about who should do the washing up. One day, instead of arguing, listen to all that they have to say and acknowledge that you can see why they are upset.

This will have quite an effect on the disagreement. It may move to resolution, or it may change tack to make you feel resentful that you have listened to your partner when they don't listen to you; and it may make them feel guilty for the same reason. This is fundamental in demonstrating that the argument is not about the washing up at all; it is about the levels of respect you have for each other and the idea of being put-upon. If you can both see this, you can begin to look at why you both feel put-upon, guilty or resentful, and where these feelings came from.

Kabbalah teaches that whatever we do in one of the four worlds will work its way through to the others. So the 'law of change' will work physically as well as mentally or emotionally.

Holistic practices such as the Alexander Technique teach that amending your posture can help on emotional levels, too. And, for any of us, it is possible to begin to change our lives by amending our physical habits.

The main benefit from addressing change is that it demonstrates to cosmic law that you are willing to have new experiences in your life. If you are feeling blocked or cannot attract the relationship you want, changing some part of your life will allow different energies to come in. Teaching yourself how to change also makes it easier to adapt when big changes in life appear to be threatening.

When we change we present a different dynamic to the outside world. You may have noticed how friends' attitudes to you change if you get a new and better job. You say you haven't changed but their perception of you is now different. People often resist change for just this reason. However, if you are not willing to change and grow then you will become dissatisfied and resentful – and try to stop others from growing too.

Adapting to the idea of change also makes you more open to the idea of examining issues within your relationships in order to solve them, instead of going round and round the same old Yesodic arguments that get you nowhere.

At the end of all this is the knowledge that patterns exist in our lives and that we are likely to run those patterns in all of our relationships. However, consciousness can always overcome habit if it is applied with knowledge and discipline. We have the gift of free will (see pages 46–59); all we have to do is use it.

Consciousness can always overcome habit if it is applied with knowledge and discipline.

LOVE, its purpose, creation and fulfilment

To people involved in spiritual work, love is the goal. But do we really understand what love is? In the same way that the Inuit have more than a dozen words for snow, perhaps we need more names for love.

Some people have a problem with the idea of unity or God being love, because they say that love must have an opposite – as in hatred. If you get rid of the idea of duality, how can you have love?

The problem there is the definition of love. If love is on the right-hand pillar, then hatred should be on the left-hand pillar. However, the Tree of Life shows that all things in duality operate in conjunction with their opposite sefirah and, when out of balance, become a part of that opposite sefirah. For example, loving someone so desperately that you cannot live without them and try to trap them into loving you back stops being Hesedic love and becomes Gevuric/Hodian.

Hatred is a cry for love and, as such, is in a strange way a part of love. We hate because we do not feel loved; not because the world does not contain love. We hate because we feel unworthy, rejected and unable to alter the situation. And if we are told (maybe through religion) that we truly are unworthy, that leads to guilt and resentment – which can be projected onto everyone else's God because that is a safe thing to do.

A kabbalistic view would be that *real* love is a merging of Hesedic loving kindness and Gevuric discernment held at Tiferet. After all, sometimes the kindest thing we can do is to say 'No' rather than 'Yes'. Love lets people go, as well as drawing them to us. It is a case of unity arising from the merging of duality on the central pillar. In that case, love *is* all that there truly is, and anything else is an imbalance.

So the purpose of love is to focus us on the idea of unity – that is, on our relationship with ourselves in conjunction with God. We create it by being in balance with ourselves and by accepting ourselves as we are; and we fulfil it by living it in the world, whether or not other people are offering us love back.

To *be* love is everything; when we are love, we are in a symbiotic relationship with God, in which God automatically reflects love back to us. So to be love means to receive love, and that is unity.

Exercise

Forgiveness

Spend a week or more over this exercise. Take a notebook and write down the names of everyone who has ever hurt you and every incident that has ever upset you from the day of your very first memory. No matter how small it was, write it down. Don't be afraid to put your loved one's name down too – and your own because there may be many things that you blame yourself for. It is important not to do this all at once because it could get very depressing. We don't generally realize how much 'baggage' of conflict, anger and grief that we carry and the realization of it is very powerful.

When you think that your list is complete, see if you can find any patterns in it. Has the same type of thing happened over and over again? If so, can you work out which sefirah within you is the one which is continually being hurt? Is it your pride? Your sexuality? Your abilities at work or learning? Is it a particular type of person who bullies you or who lets you down? If you can find a pattern and locate the sefirah concerned, endeavour to work on that aspect of conflict within you which draws this experience.

A simple way to do that is to visualize your own personal Tree of Life in front of you and to bathe that sefirah with healing water and herbs in your mind's eye, cleansing it and loving it. Using herbal remedies such as the Bach or Australian Flower tinctures can also be very helpful. However, the most important thing to do to create forgiveness is to express the desire to forgive the very first person who hurt you in each area of your life. It is the unresolved pain from that primary experience which has been following you around and recreating itself in your life in order to alert you to an old, unresolved problem.

To bring forgiveness to the situation, you can write an angel letter (see page 111) or simply write or say 'I am willing to release the past. I am willing to forgive (whoever or whatever it is)' ten times a day for 40 days. If you can bring that amount of commitment to this exercise, the situation and the bad feelings which have recreated it will dissolve and you will find that other people and incidents become much easier to release.

Higher LEVELS:
guides and helpers

There are times in life when we need all the support we can get. Kabbalah teaches that help is at hand from the higher worlds and that it is foolish to try to go it alone all the time. We have both angels and human guides constantly standing by to help us.

Everything we say or do affects the universe. As the kabbalist and alchemist Dr David Goddard says in *The Sacred Magic of the Angels*, 'The worm trodden underfoot shakes the very throne of God.'

If we are in genuine danger, help from above is offered immediately; but, when it comes to smaller things, our guides will not interfere without being asked, because that would negate our gift of free will (see pages 46–59). A child learning to walk has to totter and fall so that he or she can learn what *not* to do, as well as what must be done. It is up to us to call for assistance if we need a hand; it is part of our learning process to realize that we can – and must – seek guidance. If we were more awake and less proud, our lives might well be a lot easier.

Kabbalah specifies that angels are focused beings of pure energy, who have been created by God for a specific purpose.

The different levels of ANGELS

There are two distinct types of helpers on whom we can call: human and non-human. To a kabbalist, the word 'angel' refers to the non-human type. This makes angelology in Kabbalah very different in tone from many of the angel books and workshops around today, because Kabbalah specifies that angels are focused beings of pure energy, who have been created by God for a specific purpose and are incapable of free will. But angel teachers such as Diana Cooper, Doreen Virtue and Terry Lynn Taylor believe that an angel *does* have free will and will help us voluntarily as a guide or guardian and will respond to our requests and appeals. Both views are equally valid; the word 'angel' in both Hebrew and Greek simply means 'messenger', and discarnate guardians, guides and helpers (that is, human ones who have lived on Earth and are now dead) are just as much messengers as the non-human kind of angel.

The levels of ARCHANGELS

In most spiritual traditions the word 'archangel' is used generically to cover a wide range of celestial beings.

Kabbalah teaches that Lucifer was the greatest of the archangelic beings, and he thought himself superior to humankind. God asked all the angels and archangels to acknowledge Adam as the highest of spirits, but Lucifer refused to bow to the first human.

The Holy One then set up a contest between Adam and Lucifer to name the creatures of the world. Whoever could do that best would be judged the greatest. Adam named the animals easily, but Lucifer – as a being with no ability to invent or create – could not compete and was humiliated in front of all the other angels and archangels. He left the heavens (with some of his companions) and vowed to be man's enemy for eternity.

His first 'success' was the temptation of Eve in the Garden of Eden, but Lucifer (nowadays usually known as Satan) is still around to tempt us all the time. He lost his link to God – whom he loved greatly – and Kabbalah teaches that he wants to take revenge on humanity by stopping us reaching divinity too. He walks the path between Yesod and Tiferet, tempting us with distractions and devilish thoughts. Ironically, by doing so, he is still God's greatest servant because everyone's mettle must be tested on the spiritual path and, if we cannot outwit Lucifer, we are not ready to proceed.

The Lucific principle is not ugly and repulsive, as many people believe – for Lucifer was a great and beautiful being. Even now his form of temptation comes in attractive guises. Sometimes when we see the face of someone who has done great evil, in the name of goodness or religion, it will appear to be beautiful. This is known as the Lucific principle, and that is how Lucifer catches his converts.

Angels and Archangels are not the cuddly, chubby manifestations that we see in art; instead, they are powerful beings of light, each with a particular job to do.

COSMIC BEINGS
ON JACOB'S LADDER

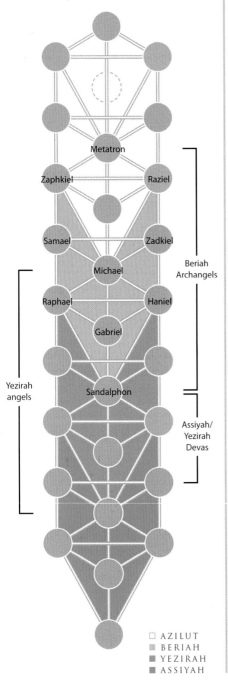

Metatron

Zaphkiel   Raziel

Samael   Zadkiel

Michael

Raphael   Haniel

Gabriel

Sandalphon

Beriah
Archangels

Yezirah
angels

Assiyah/
Yezirah
Devas

□ AZILUT
■ BERIAH
■ YEZIRAH
■ ASSIYAH

Kabbalah teaches that Lucifer's place in the cosmos was taken by Metatron, who was once known as Enoch and is the world's first fully realized human being. As such, he has the free will of a human merged with the spiritual power of an archangel. He is mentioned in Genesis, and several important metaphysical books bear his name. Enoch/Metatron has the ability to appear on Earth at will, and it was he (as Melchizedek, King of Salem) who initiated Abraham and Sarah into the Teaching. Kabbalists are taught that Enoch was also the prophet Elijah and has appeared in many other guises over the millennia.

Metatron stands at the Keter of Beriah/Tiferet of Azilut (see left), the highest point achievable before final union with God. His cosmic counterpart is Sandalphon, the archangelic being at the Malkhut of Beriah/Tiferet of Yezirah, who is his mirror image and represents the way Metatron appears to people on Earth.

All the other archangels have names ending in 'el' – meaning 'of God'. At the Hokhmah and Binah of Beriah are Raziel (the Revelation of God) and Zaphkiel (the Understanding of God). Raziel is said to be the archangel who gave the 'book of secrets' – the first manifestation of the teachings of Kabbalah – to Adam and Eve as they left Eden. In the places of Gevurah and Hesed are Samael (Cosmic Evil) and Zadkiel (Cosmic Good). The equivalent sefirot in Assiyah (the physical world) are 'decay' and 'growth'.

Samael is different from Satan, and here Cosmic Evil refers to the process of pure destruction. From this comes the idea of demons, but Kabbalah teaches that the demonic principle itself is not necessarily 'bad'. Demons break things down, and that is a vital component in life and death; they bring decay, and from decay comes new growth – we need compost for a fertile garden. All things die and decay to make way for the new to grow.

So, at the level of Beriah, 'evil' is pure destruction rather than wilful unkindness. However, it is this energy that can be pulled down to give power to those who wish to use its energy for wrongdoing. God will not stop that happening, because we have the right to make whatever choices we want. The forces of good will always outdo the forces of evil in the long run, because the whole of creation is angled towards unity and ultimate good. On the more positive side, it is Samael who breaks down opposition to projects; who separates warring nations and ends destructive disputes.

Zadkiel, as Cosmic Good, is a pure force for creation. As we have seen with the expansive energies of Jupiter at the Hesed of Yezirah, constant expansion is just as out-of-balance as constant contraction. Each archangel without its counterpart to temper and balance its power would prove a dangerous force indeed.

At the Tiferet of Beriah stands Great Michael (Captain of the Host). His name means 'like unto God' and he is in charge of the angelic forces that fight for order over chaos. He is also associated with marriage and legitimate ambition. Raphael (archangel of healing and communication) stands at Hod, with Haniel (archangel of beauty, harmony and romance) at Nezach.

Gabriel is placed at the Yesod of Beriah – which is also the Da'at of Yezirah – and he demonstrates perfectly the merging point of these two sefirot. Da'at is the pathway between worlds, a place where knowledge can be transmitted across levels or lost in darkness. It is also known as the place of the 'long dark night of the soul'. As the great messenger to holy prophets, Gabriel slips between the worlds of Beriah and Yezirah, able to take on form at will and appear to those who desire to see him.

The COSMIC ORDER of archangelic beings

None of these great archangels stands alone at its particular level; each is simply the primary angelic being in charge of hosts of other similar beings. How these fit on the Tree of Life was formulated through the work of the 13th-century Catholic scholar Thomas Aquinas, who merged the kabbalistic work of Dionysius the Areopagite with that of the Greek philosopher Aristotle.

Dionysius first claimed to be a disciple of Paul of Tarsus (Acts 17: 34), but later turned out to be a Christian mystic from around the year 500 CE, who had been deeply influenced by the Athenian Neoplatonic school of mysticism. He was the author of three long treatises (*The Divine Names, The Celestial Hierarchies* and *The Ecclesiastical Hierarchy*) and one short treatise (*The Mystical Theology*).

According to Dionysius, the cosmic order of archangelic beings is:

- ○ SERAPHIM
- ○ CHERUBIM
- ○ THRONES
- ○ DOMINIONS
- ○ POWERS
- ○ VIRTUES
- ○ PRINCIPALITIES
- ○ ARCHANGELS
- ○ ANGELS

The Archangel Gabriel was the angelic being who told Mary that she would become the mother of Jesus. Gabriel is usually depicted carrying lilies.

COSMIC ORDER OF ARCHANGELIC BEINGS

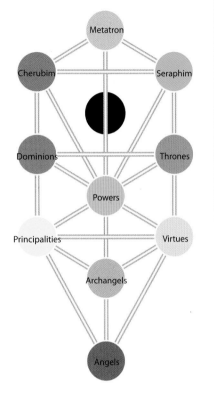

METATRON stands at the lead of the archangelic world of Beriah as the link point between Divinity and Spirit.

SERAPHIM are the angels closest to the throne of God. There are said to be four of them (equating to the Four Holy Beasts of Christian theology) and they are so bright that not even the other celestials can look directly at them. Their name means 'ardour' and they circle the throne of God chanting the words 'holy, holy, holy'.

CHERUBIM are definitely *not* the cute, chubby children of popular belief and artistic representation. The word 'cherubim' means 'fullness of knowledge' and these are the celestials who understand the workings of God and the Divine Science of Existence.

THRONES are also known as the Ophanim. Their name comes from their depiction as 'God's chariot' in which the Holy One would sit. They carry out God's desires and their primary characteristics are peace, submission and humility.

DOMINIONS are also known as Hashmallim. They execute the commands of God and regulate the duties of the lower angels. They make sure that the cosmos works in balance.

POWERS are archangels who maintain the border between divinity and Yezirah, and guard the Divine from evil thoughts and spirits. They are at the forefront in the 'war against evil' and are the great protectors and fighters of the cosmos.

VIRTUES are also known as the Tarshishim and the Malakim. Virtues command the natural world, the stars and planets, the weather and the seasons.

PRINCIPALITIES watch over mortals and their places of residence: villages, towns, cities. They rule religion and politics and ensure that the 'everyday' tasks of the angelic world below are carried out correctly.

Although we use the word 'ARCHANGEL' as a generic description of the angelic beings of Beriah, Gabriel is the only 'true' archangel that we know. The celestial beings at this level are the ones entrusted with messages and missions for humanity. They are the great guardians of states, leaders and people, who are working for the good of the world, and they rally with Michael and the other powers if there is a rebellion of evil.

The word 'ANGEL' comes from the Hebrew *mal'akh*, meaning 'messenger'; the Persian *angaros*, or 'courier'; the Greek *angelos*, meaning 'messenger'. These are the 'ordinary' celestials who carry messages between humankind, the higher ranks of celestials and God. They mirror the goodness of God and are sent to guide and protect individuals and homes.

TRUE ANGELS

A 'real' angel in Kabbalah is an energy form created for a specific purpose: a Nezachian angel to kick-start the seasons; an Hesedic angel of laughter; a Hodian angel of work or of creative play, and so on. There are angels of light, angels of love, angels of peace, angels of ritual, angels of darkness.

As humans are children of God, we create constantly – by thinking, speaking, writing or drawing. It is quite possible for us to create an angelic thought form to act as a guardian – or as an invisible friend – by imagining a being who is constactly with us as support and guide. That friend will do exactly what we tell it to and will appear as real as a human being; it just will not manifest in the physical world. Kabbalah teaches that the invisible friends of some children are discarnate human soul guides, and some are self-created angels. If a child has a particularly destructive and unpleasant 'friend', then it may be what is known as a *dibbuk* – an Earth-bound soul who has latched on to some friendly energy. This problem can usually be solved by praying that the child's own guardians will take the soul to its appropriate level or give the child protection.

Kabbalah teaches that when we create an angelic form through thought, it will strengthen when we give energy to it and weaken when we do not. Some people call these forms 'entities' and they may be good or bad, according to the thoughts that create them. When we stop using them, they fade away and the energy is reabsorbed into something else.

Occasionally other people's thought-forms will stay behind when they die or move on, or will impinge on others, like ghosts. You may feel a cold presence in a house or get an uneasy feeling in a doorway. These thought-forms fade away eventually if they are not 'fed' with energy, but it may be a good idea to cleanse a new home using a Native North American smudge stick or an atomizer spray of flower essences, to stop old energy forms from sticking.

Therapists who work from home and people working at health centres need to carry out regular cleansings because of the energetic 'stuff' that clients drop and leave behind when they receive healing.

SOUL GUIDES

Kabbalah teaches that our guides and guardians are usually souls who know us well. They may have been former lovers, parents or friends, and generally they are just one step further up the ladder than we are, so they have slightly more sense than us – and the ability to look at the big picture.

As humans are children of God, we create constantly – by thinking, speaking, writing or drawing.

If there is a specific job to be done, an 'expert' guide may be allotted to us for a short period of time and, if we are showing signs of doing well, we may even share a guide with other people because we do not need too much assistance from above.

Guides live in Yezirah, for only there can they adopt forms that we can see, sense or hear. All 'angels', whether human or not, are capable of presenting themselves to us in a form that we are willing to comprehend in order to make life easier for us. Because of images passed down to us through our churches, this usually incorporates two wings, an anthropomorphic or feminine appearance, flowing clothing and no feet.

However, kabbalists believe that an 'angel' can also present itself as a dog, a colour of light, a tramp or even as graffiti on a wall; it has no problem with any kind of manifestation. It could also turn up as a demon, if that would help.

Contacting GUIDES

Our guides usually contact us at times when we are still and receptive: in sleep or in meditation. However, the occasional instruction or warning will get through to us in the form of intuition, even on a busy day at work.

In kabbalistic terms, a guide – being human – is as much a child of God as we are. Guides are capable of making mistakes, but because they have the wider view of our life-plan, they are usually able to advise us well. 'Real' angels, on the other hand, are the *servants* of God and of humankind. That is their purpose and their joy.

Earth spirits, fairies and goblins

Kabbalistic archangels operate in Beriah, while angels operate throughout Yezirah. Angels start with the Earth spirits, or devas, that inhabit all of nature. Fairies, goblins, gnomes and elves are all real, but (like all beings that exist only in Yezirah) they are hard to see and do not encourage human contact or intervention. They are simply doing their job very nicely, thank you. Some of them are naturally mischievous, but the antics of the fairies in William Shakespeare's *A Midsummer Night's Dream* are rather beyond their sphere.

One of the reasons people talk to plants is to let the devas of those plants know what is likely to happen to them. As angelic beings, devas will serve humans if given a direct order from the children of God; so if we inform them that their plant is going to be moved or pruned, they will cooperate. The deva

Earth spirits are a part of the driving force of nature, in rocks, water and vegetation.

of a weed will obviously object to being pulled up because it is not interested in having an ordered garden, but only in survival. However, we can still tell it what will happen and thereby lessen the shock.

Nature devas are very basic and earthy. They are attracted by the energies of love and hate because they do not experience them themselves, and they will actually egg us on if we are quarrelling or feeling lustful in their kingdom. Mountains, rivers, valleys and forests also have devas – and so do elements such as wind, rain and fire. States and countries too have their angelic beings – and each one has a different essence that becomes quite apparent when we cross boundaries or borders.

Young children instinctively know about Earth-children devas because they are still attuned to the other levels of Yezirah, so if children tell us they have seen a fairy, they are probably telling the truth, even if the 'seeing' was done with an inner eye.

Angels and devas vary in size and power according to their purpose, and they are created, trained and dissolve according to need. Gaia, the spirit of the Earth, is an angel, as are the spirits of all the other planets in the solar system. The Sun, however, is the equivalent of an archangelic being – at quite a different level.

How to ACCESS angels and archangels

Kabbalists are taught that it is not wise to mess with angels unless we are using them for their correct purpose – as messengers. They will carry petitions to God and bring answers back; they will contact other people for us; and they will obey our commands, as children of the Creator. But if we summon an angel, we have taken a lot of responsibility on our heads. And if we consider the fact that we are calling something that may be – energetically – the size of a planet, then it is worth erring on the side of caution.

It is also taught that it is improper for us to summon a busy angelic being on a whim, and then forget about it because the telephone rings and distracts us. If we have commanded it, a true angel will not leave until we, our guide or God dismisses it. Many people report summoning the great archangels Michael, Gabriel or Raphael to help them; to a kabbalist, that is rather like asking the Sun and the bright stars Alpha Centauri and Sirius into your living room simultaneously.

Fortunately, our guides are very helpful to us in this respect, and kabbalistic understanding suggests that they are happy to bring us an inkling of that

If children tell us that they have seen a fairy, they are probably telling the truth, even if the 'seeing' was done with an inner eye.

Great Michael, the Captain of the Host, is not to be summoned lightly. His power is equivalent to the heat and light of the Sun.

celestial power to be used for our higher good. And, if we do get distracted, they can send the power back for us – they want to help us and do not want to see us stressed.

It is fine to say, 'Great Michael send me protection', because your guide and Michael's helpers (and he has many) will refer the query up to him and he will then refer it on to God. That is what angelic beings do – they will not make the decision to help you or not themselves, because they cannot. If it is deemed to be for your highest good, the answer 'Yes' will come back in less than a nano-second, and Michael will delegate back down the line to smaller angelic beings and to your own guides. You will get an essence of Michael's energy – but kabbalists are taught that they are only fooling themselves if they believe they are dealing face-to-face with the Captain of the Host.

There are ways of petitioning the great angels, but it is best to have a go at contacting God directly first. You can get through to God at first hand – just get yourself to Tiferet (by relaxing until everyday concerns no longer have the power to distract you) and talk. Prayer is talking to God, and meditation is listening for the answer.

God will listen to your petition, decide yes or no, and delegate some appropriate angelic help to sort out the problem in hand – and will know better than you what really is needed. Incidentally, when people say that God did not answer their prayers, it may well be that the prayer did not get through because they were not focused in Tiferet when they sent it, or that there was a reply but they simply were not listening. Of course, sometimes, the answer to a specific question will have been: 'Sorry, but no'.

Oddly enough, an impassioned or desperate plea will be sent from Tiferet automatically because, once we are that distraught, we let go of the illusion of control and leave Yesod behind. We know we cannot do anything else to help ourselves, so the ego is quite at a loss and will let Tiferet take over.

The sacred angelic tradition of the western world (as described by Dr David Goddard in *The Sacred Magic of the Angels*) teaches that specific angels, archangels and celestials can be petitioned directly on certain days of the week, using particular coloured candles, paper and pens and writing in one of two angelic languages, known as the 'Theban Script' or the 'Passing of the River Script'. This may, of course, be made so complicated to try and put us off – commitment and determination are necessary in spiritual work, and we should not even think about contacting the higher worlds unless we are willing to put in the time and energy required, and ready to hear the answer that is right for us.

Each celestial being has a designated series of signs, one of which they will send to us if God's answer to our petition is 'Yes'. We cannot miss the signs when they come; producing a chameleon in the centre of London, for example, might seem a tough call to us, but is quite easy for an angel.

It all sounds very complex, but don't lose heart, because guides and angels can be approached in a much simpler way, too. An 'angel letter' (see below) will usually sort out a specific problem between two people by raising it to the level of Keter so that it can be dealt with by our higher selves. Angel letters have been known to bring messages from departed loved ones; to resolve issues at work; and to clear up misunderstandings with ease.

There is the true story of a woman who had a pregnancy terminated more than 40 years ago. She grieved over the decision and found it hard to forgive herself for many years, even though she went on to marry happily and have three children. She wrote an angel letter to the soul of the child who was aborted, asking it to forgive her and – if it were alive in the world and was willing to do so – to send her a message.

Three days later she was woken at 7 a.m. by a phone call from her youngest son, who was living and working in China. He told her that he had had a vivid dream in which she had been crying, because she thought she had hurt him – and he felt he had to telephone immediately to ask his mother what was the matter and to tell her that he was absolutely fine.

A word of caution: you are not going to get help from the angels or your guides if you ask for it gratuitously, because you cannot be bothered to do the work that is necessary or do not want to handle a tricky situation. Asking for help to get you passed over at a meeting in the office when you have not researched an assignment is out of order; so is asking for help to make someone else stop doing something that troubles you. The help is there for *you*, and not for interfering with others.

Don't despair; you can still ask for help with the assignment itself, and you may find that some time is cleared before the meeting in which you can catch up sufficiently to make amends; but, if you choose to waste that time doing something else, then you are on your own. If someone else's behaviour is bothering you and you ask for help, you will be offered strength to withstand it and guidance on how to avoid such situations in the future. However, you do have to listen for the advice and act on it – and it may well go against your natural inclinations. Once you act, then the irritant may stop – either because your previous behaviour was a part of the problem, or because you no longer need that irritation in your life.

Angel letters have been known to bring messages from departed loved ones, to resolve issues at work, and to clear up misunderstandings.

Exercise
Tuning in to your guide

If you do not know how to contact your guide or how to tune in to what he or she is trying to tell you, then it is helpful to create a thought-form for your guide to use in order to get through to you. The problem is not that they are not talking to you; but that you do not know how to listen.

Imagine a man or a woman whose image you like, from an era that you are fond of, and ask your guide if it will use that image to contact you. Then your Yesod will be comfortable with the idea and open to communication. When your guide needs to contact you, it can slip the image of that person into your mind so that you become receptive to a message.

One objection to this kind of thought-form is usually: 'But I'll only be imagining it; it won't be my real guide.' It is interesting, when you try the practice, to note how long it is before your 'imagination' starts giving you advice that you would never have thought of – or praises you when you would usually be beating yourself up. Your guides do all they can to get through; you are the one who actively stops them.

Exercise
Writing an 'angel letter'

Fill in the appropriate spaces in the angel letter given below to create your own personalized letter:

An angel letter to the Higher Self of: _____
Carried in love by the Angels of God

Dear _____

The purpose of this letter is to dissolve all unhelpful, angry and grievous links between us so that we may both move on to a greater good. I understand that both my Higher Self and yours are working for this result.

I appreciate: *[write here details of the good experiences between you]*_____
_____
_____
_____

I am upset about: *[write here details of the unhappy experiences between you]*__
_____
_____
_____

My wish for us both is: *[write here the outcome you would like – one that would benefit both sides*
*in the dispute]*_____
_____
_____
_____

The Spirit within me forgives you for any ill-will, misunderstanding, anger or hatred between us. The Spirit in you forgives me for any ill-will, misunderstanding, anger or hatred between us. You are free to be yourself; I am free to be myself. All things are cleared up between us now and for ever. Amen.

Signed: _____

Now fold and address this letter to the person (or situation) concerned. Keep it in a special place for up to two weeks. Your intuition will tell you when it has gone. Then burn the piece of paper – releasing the energy to the Divine.

So you want to be a
KABBALIST?

Kabbalah is about *you*. How you respond to every single concept or diagram in this book tells you about your own inner and outer beliefs and patterns. Understanding and using the diagrams can give you the tools you need to change your life.

The spiritual work of the kabbalist is to reflect God's image back to the Divine. In effect, God experiences the world through your senses and acts in the world through you. It doesn't comment; It doesn't interfere; It just observes. God does not have an ego problem, and It is in this relationship with you for the long run. As far as God is concerned, there is plenty of time for you to work out who you really are and what you truly want.

Spiritual discipline is just like any other form of training; it requires you to dedicate time and effort towards stretching your mind/emotions/body. If you had been born into the 'perfect' family where you had not picked up any ego habits of lack, resentment, anger or boredom, you might get away without doing any spiritual work. It is not that God or the universe is not offering you knowledge and wisdom at every step; it is that you have forgotten how to tune in.

All of us tend towards one particular way of following the spiritual path, whether it is kabbalistic or not. In accordance with the three triads circling Yesod, we are predominantly thinkers, feelers or actors and we will prefer the 'way of contemplation', the 'way of devotion' or the 'way of action'.

The most important thing is to keep sight of the goal, rather than the techniques, otherwise we may end up worshipping the map instead of following the Path.

The art of DETACHMENT

Kabbalists are taught that at the level of Tiferet they are able to experience life from a detached point of view. This does not mean that you no longer care about what goes on in the world, or in your own life, but that you can observe the wider picture.

For example, a kabbalistic student will often be given an exercise to observe the news from a detached point of view for a week. He or she is encouraged to watch world events without experiencing emotions such as anger, indignation or pity. Where such emotions arise spontaneously, the student is asked to work out which part of their Tree of Life is affected and why – this comes with experience, as you learn to recognize which part of you is reacting or responding to an external situation.

In Kabbalah, if there is a crisis before you, the task is to answer these four questions:

○ Is it real (that is, is it a proven threat rather than conjecture or 'scare tactics')?
○ Does it actually concern you or yours?
○ Can you do something about it?
○ Can you help anyone else do something about it?

If the answer to these questions is 'No', then developed kabbalists would turn their attention away from the crisis. This is not callousness; it is because they do not want to add further negative energy to a situation which is already bad enough. They would prefer to conserve their time and energy for a crisis on which they *can* offer positive help.

Of course, those kabbalists who are also trained healers can send healing to a difficult situation that is discussed on the news. However, the secret is to do that – and then let go of the result.

For the student of Kabbalah it is enough to try and ensure that we do not spend a lot of time engaging in fruitless and negative situations, because that will dissipate our own energy and add more power to what is already happening. We are here to learn, develop ourselves and help others wherever we can. But, if we cannot assist in the current situation, we are taught to move on to another situation where we can.

Spiritual discipline is just like any other form of training; it requires you to dedicate time and effort towards stretching your mind/body/emotions.

Kabbalah wants you to have an opinion; wants you to talk things through and agree or disagree. That is how it remains a living tradition.

Understanding the WORLD today

Kabbalah teaches that all countries and nations come under karmic law in the same way that individuals and families do. All countries also have their own angelic being as a supervising agent – and they are subject to astrological law, according to the date when the country was inaugurated, ratified or founded.

The United Kingdom, for example, is ruled by a Capricorn Sun (set by the date of ratification of the countries of England, Northern Ireland, Scotland and Wales into one union in January 1801. This makes the people of that nation naturally cautious; concerned with structure and law; slightly pessimistic; but very kind, once their outer stiffness and formality have been breached.

The United States is ruled by a Cancer Sun (designated by the signing of the Declaration of Independence in July 1776), which makes it a 'mother figure' in the world, caring and nurturing its own and its allies, and fiercely preventing any perceived security threat from breaching its outer shell.

To the kabbalist, international crises are learning tools to enable humanity to choose to respond, rather than react. Although it is good to find a peaceful solution, no developed kabbalist would automatically be a pacifist because that would mean aligning him- or herself with a view that might not be appropriate to all situations.

The brief for the kabbalist is to observe and assess from the level of Tiferet, rather than react from Yesod; and to observe where the karma of nations may be being replayed to them. For example, British rule in her overseas colonies has had the natural result that Britain is now responsible for a large multi-cultural population within her own shores.

It is also interesting to observe countries such as China or Russia that have moved on from imperial rule – but whose communist leaders have behaved in almost exactly the same way as the emperors or tsars who preceded them, showing that little had been learnt in the process of revolution.

How to find a deeper understanding of KABBALAH

There are many good books on Kabbalah, but you cannot truly understand your kabbalistic self without engaging in the oral tradition. This is easier than it sounds at first: just discussing a book with a friend is an excellent start. Kabbalah wants you to have an opinion; wants you to talk things through and agree or disagree. That is how it remains a living tradition.

By far the best way to study Kabbalah is in a group. Such groups exist all over the world; some of them are large and others small, but they all have one thing in common – they have *one* leader at any one time. There may be many wise people in the group, and the role of leader may change from session to session, but one person always has to take the place of Tiferet to act as chairman or chairwoman, in order to keep members working at a level above Yesod. If this does not happen, the meeting will degenerate into chat, with nothing new being learnt.

Many kabbalistic groups are led by a man and a woman working together, with each taking a pivotal role in turn. Either person can take the place of Tiferet of the group at any given time, with the other acting as an assistant to Tiferet when not assuming that role. It may be that the man opens the meeting and starts the discussion of a particular subject, and the woman takes over later to lead a meditation and the discussion that follows. If the two cannot work together, allowing the power to pass naturally between them, then the group will not work correctly.

Because the kabbalistic tradition works on distinct structures, these are open to multiple interpretations that may be debated for hours in a good kabbalistic group. You can look at the Tree of civilization; the Tree of a particular relationship; the Tree of a business; the Tree of the characters on a television show; the Tree of a football team; or the Tree of yourselves. It can be a transpersonal debate and at the same time have complete relevance to your own life. An example would be charting the story of the Exodus from Egypt on the Tree, and then looking at the levels of slavery and freedom in our own lives. It can be fascinating to see how the 'Egyptian world' of problems can become a trap that it is too scary for us to break out of today – or even to see. And we can observe that the temptation to turn back is strongest when we are in the 'wilderness' – or are feeling lost, lonely or uncomfortable in new situations.

Group discussions are there to offer us alternative views and support. We can help each other to see more clearly and to break through old, out-of-date modes of behaviour.

Working with companions: running your own KABBALISTIC group

A kabbalist *can* study on his or her own, but after a year or so it may become a rather limiting experience and, on your own, it is hard to have the necessary strength, discipline and support to be consistent.

Working in a group is the best way to understand Kabbalah. One person must lead each group, taking the place of Tiferet to hold the energy of the meeting.

SCHOOL OF KABBALAH

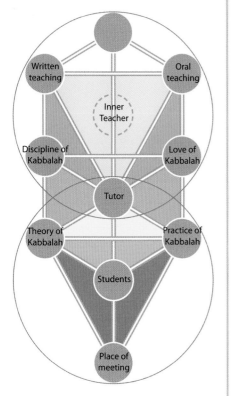

Kabbalistic gatherings of companions come together from all races and creeds in order to study together and help each other with friendship and support in everyday life. The ideal starting point for a group is seven people – one for each of the sefirot below the supernal triad – because smaller groups tend to become more like personal therapy sessions or study groups. A wider range of views is needed to keep the discussion alive.

Companions are not hard to find; the odd word at a dinner party or in the office will draw together people with spiritual beliefs. However, a distinct kabbalistic group is often quite elusive. There is a kabbalistic saying that a group should be hard to enter and easy to leave, in order to ensure that only those who truly want to work with the tradition join. Fair-weather members can be disruptive to any spiritual group. However, if you can find a kabbalistic workshop, then it normally follows that there will be a group nearby – all you have to do is ask. But, if you cannot find one, there is no prohibition on starting one yourself.

All you need in order to run your own kabbalistic group is a committed number of people who are interested in using the Tree of Life and Jacob's Ladder as points of reference on their spiritual path. The Tree of a spiritual group shows how such a gathering would work (see left), with the students at Yesod and the tutor at Tiferet. First, you need a meeting place, a tutor (probably you!) and students. As the group continues to meet, it will develop its own ideals and interpretation of the teaching, which will be stored in the side triads and will colour how the group sees itself and reponds to the outside world.

The tutor only needs to be half a step further on than the rest of the group, to be able to give a little guidance on the workings of the tradition. However, he or she does have to be aware of the projections that people put on their spiritual teacher, and must work hard to be impartial in all situations. Some of the group will love you and others will resent you. As long as you are doing the job to the best of your ability and have not fallen into the trap of pride, any issues concerning the leadership will mostly be a projection of their problems concerning authority – although these can still be challenging to deal with.

If you are prepared to commit to running a group, help will come to you from above and, when questions are asked of you at a meeting, answers will come via your inner teacher (through Da'at). You may well amaze yourself!

Once you are meeting as a group, you can establish a structure showing how you want to work, with the emphasis on contemplation, ritual or devotion (see page 117) – or a combination of all three.

CONTEMPLATION

Contemplation can take the form of studying texts for discussion or focusing on a particular subject that members should observe during the time between meetings. A subject such as 'detachment' can generate a wealth of conversation and revelation, as you all talk about experiences that have called on you to be neutral and focused in Tiferet, when you wanted to react from Yesod or from the conditioning of your emotional and intellectual side triads. The news and television also offer wonderful examples of where people are capable of 'waking up' or not. The group may note how a newsreader tends to hand over to a reporter or interviewee for 'reaction', as opposed to considered, detached opinion.

The subject can be expanded to observe where detachment becomes apathy or even cruelty, as in the case of someone deliberately disregarding the feelings of others when acting in a certain way – and the group can assess where the point of balance is and how they can hold on to that point in their own lives. Contemplation also involves thought and discussion on ritual and devotion (see below). Sharing experiences and plotting them on the Tree is at the heart of it all – and it can be incredibly rewarding.

RITUAL

Ritual can take many forms and, although people who have left their conventional faith often oppose the idea, the need for a physical expression of spirituality tends to creep up on us after a while. Kabbalists can make the Tree with their body (see page 22) to experience the levels within them, or create a simple kabbalistic service of their own.

Kabbalists believe that many religious rituals, such as the old Catholic Mass, were structured on the Tree of Life, and it is quite easy to structure your own services, which will work because they address all the levels:

- ○ MALKHUT is the place where you hold the service.
- ○ YESOD is the people taking part.
- ○ HOD is the written word – some inspirational reading.
- ○ NEZACH is an active principle, such as making the Tree with your body.
- ○ TIFERET is the place of remembrance, of gratitude for life and prayer.
- ○ GEVURAH is the acknowledgement of mistakes, unkindnesses and ideas that did not work.
- ○ HESED is the forgiveness of self and others for all errors.

A subject such as 'detachment' can generate a wealth of conversation and revelation.

A candle contains all four elements – solid and liquid wax, gas around the wick and fire.

○ DA'AT is the place of 'communion' where we speak directly to God and listen for the reply.

○ BINAH is a time of acceptance and understanding of what has gone before (perhaps another reading).

○ HOKHMAH is the time for speaking about the experience and sharing it with others.

○ KETER is the point of acting on what has been learnt or received out in the everyday world.

Alternatively, you can recreate the essence of the Sabbath Eve service of light, wine, water and bread representing the four worlds, which is kabbalistic in origin and honoured throughout Judaism. At the beginning of your meeting, light candles with a blessing for Azilut, and inhale the scent of incense for Beriah. After the meeting wash your hands for Yezirah, and then ground yourself in Assiyah with a shared snack.

Ritual also includes action, so you could hold meetings at sacred places in order to understand the links between traditions and faiths; and at places where the Tree of Life has established itself in the form of design, whether or not that was done consciously.

Many of the great cathedrals of the world, particularly those built in the 12th to 14th centuries, were based either on the Tree of Life or on Jacob's Ladder. In the 'Golden Age' of Spain during the 13th century the intelligentsia (comprising Jews, Muslims and Christians) often worked together to understand each other's traditions and techniques. Masons, too, had great spiritual knowledge. The great cathedral at Chartres is an excellent example of a church that was built to a sacred design – in this case the Tree of Life, with the entrance at Malkhut, the main altar at Tiferet and the Grand Altar at Da'at. Chartres also incorporates esoteric stories and astrological signs in its great windows and doors, and has an astrological clock placed at Hokhmah; the great maze or labyrinth on the floor denotes Yesod.

DEVOTION

Devotion usually involves prayer, song or meditation. There is a fine line between contemplative and devotional meditation, but the former is easier for beginners and those who have problems clearing their minds totally.

A guided meditation takes the participants up through the levels of Yezirah to touch the Kingdom of God. The truly devotional aspect is the time given in the middle of the meditation for each individual to sit in silence for their own communion with God. After the meditation, group members can discuss their own experiences and assess how comfortable and relaxed they are with different aspects of themselves within their own Tree of Life.

In a kabbalistic meditation, landscape generally denotes the vegetable level; animals represent the 'animal soul' of the Awakening Triad; and the first human met on the path represents the ego. Challenges and delights along the path represent different levels within us and, throughout the meditation, there are opportunities (such as dreams or gifts from people whom we meet) for our unconscious to give us messages we might not otherwise receive.

The importance of the ORAL tradition

An oral tradition ensures that a system remains alive. Meeting and discussing Kabbalah constantly adds to the knowledge of tradition, and bringing in new people with new views gives kabbalists fresh insights into life. Kabbalistic groups either thrive or fade away as the need arises. They are not meant to last for ever. In an ideal world a teacher will have another, more advanced group to go to, so that he or she can continue to learn and take his or her place as a student as well as a teacher, in order to keep a sense of balance. Sometimes new groups will grow out of old ones, and often an ailing group has to close in order for a new and more vibrant one to start. In an oral tradition, it is easier to see when a group is strong or failing. The numbers of people attending may be one indication, but the quality of discussion will be the determining factor. If only theory is discussed, the group is probably not thriving.

Sometimes, when there has been a charismatic or particularly talented teacher who has died, the rest of the group will attempt to continue in the same vein. They will elect a new leader and follow the ways of the departed teacher. Usually such groups fall apart because there is no fresh impetus. In Christianity, the Jewish followers of Jesus tried to continue the teaching and had some small success for a while but then they died out. They made what could be viewed as the classic mistake in that they elected a blood relative of the previous teacher to be their new leader when it is the spiritual line not the blood line which is important in an esoteric school.

It was Paul of Tarsus who led the next generation of teachers and his teaching inspired the world even though it was quite different from the original. Paul's strengths and weaknesses including his own inner demons and his Yesodic social conditioning became what was taught as Christianity, even though it did not originate with Jesus.

We are here to learn the inner truths of love, discernment, wisdom and revelation.

Paul's letters are an excellent example of a written teaching which becomes crystallized where an oral teaching can hold its structure and move with the times. His views on women keeping silent and keeping their heads covered, for example, were the correct Greek and Roman society procedures of that time. In fact, women who went bareheaded and prophesied in the streets of Roman cities were often in danger. The cult of Cybele, the Earth Mother, was both powerful and controversial and its followers, who included self-castrated men who grew their hair long and women with their heads uncovered, were frequently attacked in the street. Therefore, Paul's teaching at that time was correct and may have saved many women's lives. In the western world of the 21st century it appears archaic because it is not based upon Universal Principles but social mores.

There is nothing in the original teaching of Jesus that cannot be placed on the Tree of Life and merge perfectly with the modern life of the 21st century. Because he was demonstrating Universal Principles his teaching was not bound by social convention.

Kabbalists believe that each and every tradition needs a regular new influx of teachers in each generation to realize this all-important point and revitalize the teaching within its original structure. Otherwise, it will crystallize and die.

It will be interesting to observe over the next generation or so whether Kabbalah stays at the forefront of spiritual work or whether, having done its job, it retreats again to become a hidden tradition. It may thrive or it may become corrupt. It may be heralded as a 'great thing' for a century or discredited. All traditions, including Kabbalah, have their 'lost' or 'dark' teachers. Most of them mean well; most of them do very little harm.

Ultimately, it does not matter whether or not a particular tradition falls or stands, because it is only the form that will have been corrupted. The structure, the Ultimate Truth, cannot be destroyed and there will always be people who will act as its custodians, whether or not the world is willing to listen.

Most people on their spiritual path meet a corrupt system or a dark teacher somewhere along the way; it is a part of the route. If you do not meet Lucifer somewhere on your path, then you are probably not heading in the right direction! One of the most important tasks is to learn discernment and how to say 'No' to whatever feels wrong or inappropriate for you – but to do so from the Soul Triad, and not from a Yesodic reaction. The secret is not to throw the baby out with the bathwater and not to blame a tradition for its teacher. We are here to learn the inner truths of love, discernment, wisdom and revelation. Once we have those safely under our belt, we will be able to find our own way.

Exercise

Painting the Tree of Life and Jacob's Ladder

An important ritual for the would-be kabbalist is to draw or paint your own Tree of Life. You can start by drawing one out on a piece of A4 (letter-size) paper; but, for those who would like to go further, here are the instructions for painting a complete Tree and Ladder on canvas with acrylic paint. You need to allow yourself two days per diagram, but it is well worth it. You can adapt the scale quite easily to make a smaller painting.

For both diagrams you will need:

- O 1 x 0.5m (40 x 20in) canvas (fairly fine-weave)
- O a piece of hardboard slightly larger in size than the canvas
- O masking tape
- O an area of floor or a table large enough to place the hardboard on and work around
- O B or HB pencil
- O long ruler
- O compass
- O black felt pen
- O acrylic paint: white, black, red, orange, yellow, green, purple, blue
- O paint brushes: one large, plus a few small.

Tape the canvas to the hardboard using small strips of masking tape down each edge so that the canvas does not move about. After placing it on the floor or table, find the centre point of the canvas (50cm/20in down and 25cm/10 in across). Using the pencil and ruler, draw a vertical line very lightly right down the middle of the canvas. Then follow the directions on the next two pages to create the two different diagrams.

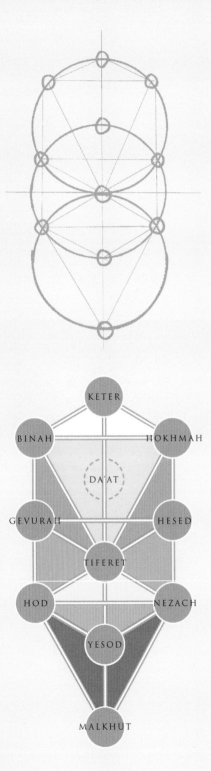

The Tree of Life

○ Set your compass to 16cm (6½in), which is the radius of the construction circles you are going to draw. Start by putting the compass needle at the centre point of the canvas and drawing a central circle lightly (see left). Then put the needle at the upper intersection of the first circle with the vertical pencil line and draw a second circle – the lower part should pass through your centre point. Do the same at the lower intersection of the centre circle with the vertical pencil line of the canvas. You should now have three overlapping circles.

○ Now set your compass to 3.5cm (1½in), which will be the radius of the sefirot. You need to draw five sefirot down the middle and three on each side, centred on the points where the circles intersect each other (at the sides) and/or the vertical pencil line (down the middle). Draw the circles, but don't draw Da'at too heavily, as it is going to have a path straight through it.

○ Next, draw the paths, which are going to be 16mm (⅔in) wide. Start with the horizontal paths. Line up the centres of the sefirot (the holes where the compass needle went) and very lightly draw a line between the sefirot. Then make a dot 8mm (⅓in) on either side of this centre line and draw in the paths as heavily as you like. Once you have drawn in the three horizontal ones, draw the vertical ones. Note that the paths down the middle go 'under' the horizontal paths, and that the one between Keter and Tiferet goes through the Da'at sefirah. Finally, put in the angled paths (making 22 in total), taking care not to put in any extra ones – or to leave any out!

○ From now on things are permanent and so, when you are sure that you have everything right, take up your compass again and put a felt-tip (or similar) pen in it and ink in the sefirot. Then ink in the paths between the sefirot. Now paint inside all the sefirot and the paths white. Once you have done that, paint Da'at (but not the path that runs through it) black, and then paint all the canvas around the tree black. This is the point at which you should finish for the day, because you will be tired by this time and the paint needs to dry.

○ The next day fill in the triads. It does not really matter what colours you use, but the traditional ones are as follows:

Red: the MALKHUT/YESOD/HOD and MALKHUT/YESOD/NEZACH triads

Orange: the YESOD/HOD/NEZACH triad

Yellow: the HOD/TIFERET/NEZACH triad

Green: the HOD/TIFERET/GEVURAH and NEZACH/TIFERET/HESED triads

Purple: the TIFERET/GEVURAH/BINAH and TIFERET/HESED/HOKHMAH triads

Blue: the TIFERET/BINAH/HOKHMAH triad

White: the BINAH/HOKHMAH/KETER triad

That might sound really complicated, but if you can follow an illustration it will make life easier.

○ Now go over the sefirot and paths again with the pens to cover any little mistakes you have made. Finally, write in the names of the sefirot and any other attributes that you wish to add – astrological planets, angels, and so on.

Jacob's Ladder

Drawing the Ladder is very similar, but there is a lot more of it. So find the centre point of the canvas, as before, and draw in the three construction circles (as for the Tree, above). There is also a whole raft of information that can be put in the sefirot. It is a time-consuming task, but it looks wonderful hanging on the wall.

○ Set your compass to 8cm (3¼in) and draw one circle at the centre point of the canvas. Then draw four more below and four above, making a total of nine.

○ Now set your compass to 2cm (¾in), which is the radius of the sefirot. There are 28 of these, plus Da'at: ten sefirot (plus Da'at) down the middle, and nine on each side. You will find that the sefirot are centred on the points where the circles intersect each other (at the sides) and/or the vertical pencil line (down the middle). Draw the circles, but don't draw Da'at too heavily, as it is going to have a path straight through it (see right).

○ Next, draw the paths, which going to be 10mm (just under ½in) wide. Start with the horizontal paths. Line up the centres of the sefirot (the holes where the compass needle went) and very lightly draw a line between the sefirot. Then make a dot 5mm (just under ¼in) on either side of this centre line and draw in the paths as heavily as you like. Once you have the nine horizontal paths in, draw in the vertical ones. Note that the ones down the middle go 'under' the horizontal paths, and that the path between Keter and Tiferet goes through Da'at. Then put in the angled paths. It is very easy to leave paths out or (more likely) put in more than you need when drawing the Ladder. You are aiming to have four overlapping trees, so if something looks wrong, it probably is!

○ The colours: the bottom tree (Assiyah) is red; the next one up (Yezirah) is purple; the next (Beriah) is blue; and the top one (Azilut) is white. That is the way it is defined in the Book of Exodus – no leeway on this one.

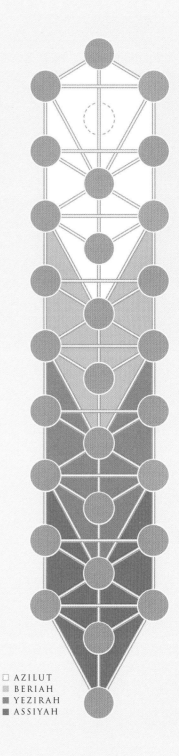

☐ AZILUT
▨ BERIAH
▧ YEZIRAH
▧ ASSIYAH

Going within and watching, hearing or sensing your reactions to the story of an inner journey can tell you much about your life's purpose.

Exercise
A kabbalistic meditation

○ Sit comfortably and close your eyes. Sense the weight and solidity of your body and of the chair you are sitting in. Make yourself as heavy as possible. Then sense the liquids within you: the blood and the lymph flowing throughout every part of your body and the saliva in your mouth. Now breathe deeply, drawing the air right down into your lungs to be distributed throughout your body by the blood, so that every cell is filled with oxygen. Feel the carbon dioxide being returned to your lungs and expel it gratefully.

○ Now feel the warmth in your body, the heat that is generated by life itself. Sense the electromagnetic field that surrounds you and its vibrant radiance: four worlds within you.

○ Imagine yourself on a hillside overlooking a valley. Is that valley fertile or barren? Is it springtime, summer, autumn or winter? Is it inhabited? Are the inhabitants friendly?

○ In the distance you can see the coastline. Start to walk towards it and notice whether you are wearing comfortable walking shoes – or are you barefoot?

○ As you cross the valley, you observe an animal that approaches you. What is it? Is it well kept? Friendly? You walk on.

○ Now you see someone waiting for you on the crest of a little hill slightly to one side of the beach area. What do they look like? They greet you. What is their attitude to you? They give you a piece of advice for your journey. Is it helpful or not?

○ Now walk down to the beach. In front of you is the sea, and you can see an island just on the horizon. This is where you are going to head in your boat. This is pulled up and moored towards the side of the beach. What state is it in? What kind of boat is it? Is it painted or unkempt?

○ You get into the boat and cast off. It knows where to go and begins to move out onto the ocean. What is the sea like? Calm or rough?

○ Night falls while you are in the boat. You lie down to sleep, but for a while you look up at the stars. As you watch the Milky Way above, you formulate a question in your mind; it is what you most want to know right now.

○ You sleep, and in your sleep you dream a dream. What is it?

○ In the morning you wake to find that your boat is just about to land on a beach of silver shingle. You take a good look around you. What is the island like? You can see that there is a hill with a small temple on it and you know that is where you are heading. You begin the climb from the beach.

○ Now you are nearly at the top of the hill. You can see the little temple. What is it like? Outside there is someone waiting for you. This is your guide. What do they look like? How do they greet you?

○ You and your guide sit down and share some food. You talk about your life and you are amazed that they know everything about you, even your innermost thoughts.

○ Once you have eaten, your guide takes you up to the temple itself and then inside. There is a courtyard area with a fountain and you are invited to wash yourself in it. When you have finished, your guide holds up a fresh, clean robe for you to wear.

○ Now you go deeper into the temple (which is much bigger inside than it appears from outside). You see three doors off to your left and three to your right. You are drawn towards one of them and you go towards it. Your guide waits outside. What is in that room?

○ You come out of the room and talk to your guide about it. They give you a very interesting insight into your experience. What is it?

○ Now you are coming up to an open area with a dome above you. It is filled with light. Your guide points out a golden disc on the floor and invites you to stand on it. You do so.

○ Slowly, softly, you are encircled by wind and feel yourself being lifted up, held by the gentlest of hands. You rise slowly towards the dome, which vanishes before you, leaving the wideness of space. You hear the faint sound of song from the celestial choirs and you are becoming a part of this great void. The feeling is both scary and full of peace. You rise higher and the song becomes louder. Then you enter into light. Pure light. There is silence. There is Presence. You are with the Divine.

○ Ask the question you formulated in the boat. And listen.

○ Once the answer has been given, you hear the song begin again and feel yourself dropping slowly out of the Presence and back into the void of sky. You are lowered gently back down, down, until you find yourself within the dome again. Down, down, until you are placed gently onto the golden disc.

○ Your guide is there, waiting for you. Together you turn and walk away, through the temple and out into the open air again. You sit in a place where you can observe the sea below you and, far away, your homeland.

○ You and your guide talk. What do you discuss?

○ Your guide tells you that it is time for you to go. They tell you that you can come back to this place any time you like. And they give you a gift. What is it?

○ You say your farewells and leave, walking back down the path to the shoreline. Your boat is waiting for you. What does your boat look like now? You climb in and it casts off. Dusk is falling. You sleep.

○ In the morning your boat lands safely on the shore of the valley coast and you get out and begin your journey home. You see the person you met in the valley the day before. Do they speak to you? Is their attitude the same?

○ Now you find yourself back where you started. Close your eyes and feel the heat and light of the electromagnetic field around you. Breathe deeply and feel the air flow through your body, feeding every cell within you. Feel the flow of the liquids within you, and now, feel the weight of your bones and the solid strength of your body. Feel the chair beneath you and your feet, firmly on the ground. Take three deep breaths and come back into the room.

INDEX

ACKNOWLEDGEMENTS IN SOURCE ORDER

Bridgeman Art Library, London/New York, 11 bottom right, 13 right, 90 bottom right/Gemaldegalerie, Berlin, Germany, 67 centre right/Museo de Bellas Artes, Seville, Spain, 29 top right/ Palazzo Ducale, Mantua, Italy 103 top right/Phillips, The International Fine Art Auctioneers,101 top right/Santa Maria della Concezione, Rome, Italy, 108 top left

Corbis UK Ltd 38 top left/Johnny Buzzerio, 87 top left/Jose Luis Pelaez, Inc. 41 top right/Laureen March, 87 right/Michael Wray, 72 top left/Roy McMahon, 96 bottom centre left/Royalty-Free, 79 top right, 125 bottom centre/Scott Roper, 63 top right

Getty Images 39 bottom right,81 bottom right,115 bottom right/ Alyson Aliano 24 top centre/Andy Sacks 74 top/Georgette Douwma 36 top/ John William Banagan 75 top right/Photodisc /Getty Images 87 centre

Octopus Publishing Group Limited 9 bottom right, 14 top centre/David Loftus, 87 top right/Gary Latham 87 centre left

top/Ian Wallace 87 top centre/Janet Foss 106 centre left/Mark Winwood 73 top right, 118 top left, 124 top left /Nasa 53 top right/Peter Myers 87 centre right bottom/Peter Pugh Cook 87 bottom right,17 bottom right, 93 bottom right/Colin Gotts 91 Top Right/Gareth Sambidge 46 centre left, 64 bottom left/ William Reavell 56 top left, 57 top right/93 bottom right, 33 bottom right, 61 bottom right, 84 top left

Rubberball Productions 5 bottom right, 46 top centre, 76 top left, 87 bottom centre left, 88 top, 112 top centre, 6 top left

Executive Editor David Alexander
Managing Editor Clare Churly
Executive Art Editor/Book Design Rozelle Bentheim
Designers Cobalt id
Production Controller Manjit Sihra